U.S. Department of
Transportation

**Federal Railroad
Administration**

Application of Welded Steel Sandwich Panels for Tank Car Shell Impact Protection

Office of Research
and Development
Washington, DC 20590

DOT/FRA/ORD-13/19

Final Report
April 2013

REPORT DOCUMENTATION PAGE

Form Approved
OMB No. 0704-0188

1. AGENCY USE ONLY (Leave blank)	2. REPORT DATE April 2013	3. REPORT TYPE AND DATES COVERED

4. TITLE AND SUBTITLE	5. FUNDING NUMBERS
Application of Welded Steel Sandwich Panels for Tank Car Shell Impact Protection	DTFR53-00-C-00012 Task Order 264
6. AUTHOR(S) and FRA COTR Michael E. Carolan, David Y. Jeong, Benjamin Perlman, Yellapu V. Murty, Shannon Namboodri, Bob Kurtz, R.K. Elzey, Satima Anankitpaiboon, Lucy Tunna, and Robert Fries	

7. PERFORMING ORGANIZATION NAME(S) AND ADDRESS(ES)	8. PERFORMING ORGANIZATION REPORT NUMBER
U.S. Department of Transportation John A. Volpe National Transportation Systems Center 55 Broadway Cambridge, MA 02142 Cellular Materials International, Inc. 1200 Five Springs Road, Suite 201 Charlottesville, VA 22902 Transportation Technology Center, Inc. 55500 DOT Road Pueblo, CO 81001	

9. SPONSORING/MONITORING AGENCY NAME(S) AND ADDRESS(ES)	10. SPONSORING/MONITORING AGENCY REPORT NUMBER
U.S. Department of Transportation Federal Railroad Administration Office of Research and Development Washington, DC 20590	DOT/FRA/ORD-13/19

11. SUPPLEMENTARY NOTES
Program Manager: Francisco González III

12a. DISTRIBUTION/AVAILABILITY STATEMENT	12b. DISTRIBUTION CODE
This document is available to the public through the FRA Web site at http://www.fra.dot.gov.	

13. ABSTRACT (Maximum 200 words)

This report describes research conducted to examine the application of sandwich structure technology to provide protection against the threat of an indenter striking the side or shell of a tank car in the event of an accident. This research was conducted in two phases over a 3-year period. Testing and analysis of flat, welded steel sandwich panels was conducted in the initial phase of the research. Based on the observations and results from that initial phase, a curved, welded steel sandwich panel was designed and built to protect the side or shell of a decommissioned liquid chlorine tank car during a full-scale impact test. Although the protective panel experienced severe damage, the commodity-carrying tank experienced only permanent deformation and did not puncture.

14. SUBJECT TERMS	15. NUMBER OF PAGES
Tank car, impact, protective panel	76
	16. PRICE CODE

17. SECURITY CLASSIFICATION OF REPORT	18. SECURITY CLASSIFICATION OF THIS PAGE	19. SECURITY CLASSIFICATION OF ABSTRACT	20. LIMITATION OF ABSTRACT
Unclassified	Unclassified	Unclassified	

NSN 7540-01-280-5500

Standard Form 298 (Rev. 2-89)
Prescribed by ANSI Std. 239-18
298-102

i

METRIC/ENGLISH CONVERSION FACTORS

ENGLISH TO METRIC	METRIC TO ENGLISH
LENGTH (APPROXIMATE)	**LENGTH** (APPROXIMATE)
1 inch (in) = 2.5 centimeters (cm)	1 millimeter (mm) = 0.04 inch (in)
1 foot (ft) = 30 centimeters (cm)	1 centimeter (cm) = 0.4 inch (in)
1 yard (yd) = 0.9 meter (m)	1 meter (m) = 3.3 feet (ft)
1 mile (mi) = 1.6 kilometers (km)	1 meter (m) = 1.1 yards (yd)
	1 kilometer (km) = 0.6 mile (mi)
AREA (APPROXIMATE)	**AREA** (APPROXIMATE)
1 square inch (sq in, in^2) = 6.5 square centimeters (cm^2)	1 square centimeter (cm^2) = 0.16 square inch (sq in, in^2)
1 square foot (sq ft, ft^2) = 0.09 square meter (m^2)	1 square meter (m^2) = 1.2 square yards (sq yd, yd^2)
1 square yard (sq yd, yd^2) = 0.8 square meter (m^2)	1 square kilometer (km^2) = 0.4 square mile (sq mi, mi^2)
1 square mile (sq mi, mi^2) = 2.6 square kilometers (km^2)	10,000 square meters (m^2) = 1 hectare (ha) = 2.5 acres
1 acre = 0.4 hectare (he) = 4,000 square meters (m^2)	
MASS - WEIGHT (APPROXIMATE)	**MASS - WEIGHT** (APPROXIMATE)
1 ounce (oz) = 28 grams (gm)	1 gram (gm) = 0.036 ounce (oz)
1 pound (lb) = 0.45 kilogram (kg)	1 kilogram (kg) = 2.2 pounds (lb)
1 short ton = 2,000 pounds (lb) = 0.9 tonne (t)	1 tonne (t) = 1,000 kilograms (kg) = 1.1 short tons
VOLUME (APPROXIMATE)	**VOLUME** (APPROXIMATE)
1 teaspoon (tsp) = 5 milliliters (ml)	1 milliliter (ml) = 0.03 fluid ounce (fl oz)
1 tablespoon (tbsp) = 15 milliliters (ml)	1 liter (l) = 2.1 pints (pt)
1 fluid ounce (fl oz) = 30 milliliters (ml)	1 liter (l) = 1.06 quarts (qt)
1 cup (c) = 0.24 liter (l)	1 liter (l) = 0.26 gallon (gal)
1 pint (pt) = 0.47 liter (l)	
1 quart (qt) = 0.96 liter (l)	
1 gallon (gal) = 3.8 liters (l)	
1 cubic foot (cu ft, ft^3) = 0.03 cubic meter (m^3)	1 cubic meter (m^3) = 36 cubic feet (cu ft, ft^3)
1 cubic yard (cu yd, yd^3) = 0.76 cubic meter (m^3)	1 cubic meter (m^3) = 1.3 cubic yards (cu yd, yd^3)
TEMPERATURE (EXACT)	**TEMPERATURE** (EXACT)
[(x-32)(5/9)] °F = y °C	[(9/5) y + 32] °C = x °F

QUICK INCH - CENTIMETER LENGTH CONVERSION

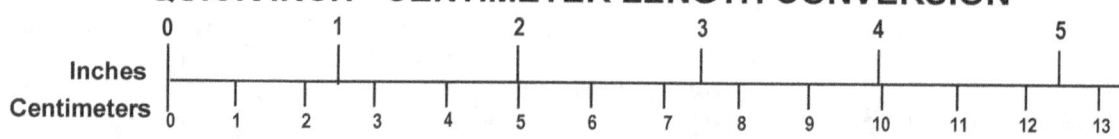

QUICK FAHRENHEIT - CELSIUS TEMPERATURE CONVERSIC

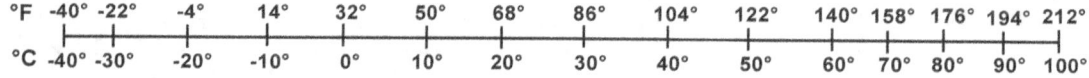

For more exact and or other conversion factors, see NIST Miscellaneous Publication 286, Units of Weights and Measures. Price $2.50 SD Catalog No. C13 10286

Updated 6/17/98

Contents

Illustrations

Tables

Executive Summary

One of the objectives of research sponsored by the Federal Railroad Administration (FRA) Office of Research and Development is to improve the transportation safety of railroad tank cars carrying hazardous materials (hazmat). This objective can be accomplished by investing resources to improve either the track infrastructure or the equipment. The focus of this report is the latter.

This report describes research conducted to examine the application of sandwich structure technology to provide protection against the threat of an indenter striking the side or shell of a tank car in the event of an accident. The principal advantages of sandwich structures are their ability to dissipate impact energy and to redistribute the impact force. The research program was conducted in two phases. The initial phase of research entailed the testing and analysis of flat, welded steel sandwich panels with different core geometries and face sheet arrangements. This research included the selection of materials based on mechanical properties such as yield strength, ultimate tensile strength, and ductility. Various manufacturing processes such as welding practices were considered in the development and application of sandwich structure technology for shell protection purposes. The research conducted in the initial phase of the program is described in detail in a previous report.

Based on the observations and results from the initial stages of research, a curved, welded steel sandwich panel was designed and built to protect the side of a decommissioned liquid chlorine tank car during a full-scale impact test. Moreover, the full-scale tank car shell impact test represented the culmination of the three-year research effort sponsored by FRA's Office of Research and Development.

Several organizations contributed to the overall research effort. The John A. Volpe National Transportation Systems Center (Volpe Center) provided technical support by conducting analytical studies, designing various tests to generate technical information to develop the protective panel, and helping to guide the overall research effort. Cellular Materials International, Inc. (CMI) was under contract with FRA to provide expertise on sandwich panels concerning such aspects as manufacturing development, fabrication processes, and evaluation of material properties. Transportation Technology Center, Inc. (TTCI) prepared for and conducted the full-scale impact test.

In the full-scale impact test conducted at the completion of this research program, a DOT105J500W specification tank car was filled with water to an outage of 10 percent and was pressurized to 100 psi. A 6-foot by 6-foot protective panel weighing approximately 900 pounds was attached to the side of the tank car. The location of the panel covered the longitudinal center of the tank at its equator. A ram car weighing 295,725 pounds impacted the center of the panel at a speed of 17.8 miles per hour (mph), which corresponds to more than 3 million foot-pounds of kinetic energy. The impact was made using an indenter with a 12-inch by 12-inch footprint. Although the protective panel experienced severe damage, the commodity-carrying tank experienced only permanent deformation and did not puncture.

Using a 6-foot by 6-foot curved panel to protect the side of a tank car is similar to using a half-height shield to protect the end or the head of a tank car. Given the dramatically improved safety performance of tank cars after head protection requirements were instituted, this similarity led to the idea of using protective panels based on sandwich structure technology to retrofit existing tank cars against the threat of side of shell impacts. A possible strategy to optimize the costs, risks, and benefits associated with shell protection might be partial protection of the tank. For example, some benefit balanced against cost and risk could be realized from protecting only the bottom half of the tank since accident statistics indicate that shell punctures are more likely to occur along the lower half of the tank. Partial protection schemes are outlined in Appendix A.

One area that remains open in terms of applying sandwich structure technology to protect railroad tank cars against shell puncture is how to effectively attach the protective panel to the tank structure. The attachments would need to be compliant or flexible in order to mitigate localized failures. Various concepts are outlined in Appendix B of this report, but ultimately the expertise and the experience of tank car manufacturers will be required to develop an appropriate design.

Absorbing and dissipating 3 million foot-pounds of energy represents a formidable challenge because the design of such a system is constrained by the maximum allowable weight and clearance standards for rail cars. The effect of weight and space budgets on designs to improve the safety performance of tank cars is discussed in previous work [6]. The protective panel designed and built for the full-scale impact test weighed approximately 900 pounds. If such panels covered the entire tank car shell, the resulting shell protection system would be well within weight and space limitations for tank cars built to 286,000-pound gross weights. The observations and results from the research described in this report suggest that sandwich structure technology can, in principle, be applied to provide protection to the tank car shell in the event of a shell impact. Moreover, protection against puncture is essential for tank cars carrying those materials with the greatest potential to harm humans and the environment if released.

1.   Introduction

Approximately two million shipments of hazmat are made by rail in North America annually [1]. Rail is recognized as the safest mode of transportation for moving large quantities of hazmat over large distances. Most rail-hauled hazmat shipments are carried in tank cars.[1] A review of accident statistics indicates that the safety performance of railroad tank cars has improved significantly over the past 25 years [2]. The improved safety trend is attributed to long-term research sponsored by the industry and the government regulatory agencies in North America, specifically the Federal Railroad Administration (FRA) and Transport Canada. Moreover, this research led to the development of thermal protection systems, double-shelf couplers, large-capacity pressure relief valves, and head protection. Subsequently, safety regulations were instituted to require these design features for particular tank cars depending on the commodity being transported.

However, accidents involving the release of hazmat from rail cars can result in property damage, environmental damage, evacuation of nearby population, injuries, and fatalities. Furthermore, the severity of some recent accidents involving the release of hazardous materials has raised attention about the crashworthiness of railroad tank cars under accident loading conditions. Table 1 lists some railroad hazmat accidents over the last decade. In five of the accidents listed in the table, the probable cause of the derailment was determined to be either a broken rail (New Brighton, PA; Oneida, NY; and Arcadia, OH) or a failure at a rail joint (Minot, ND, and Painesville, OH). In the two most recent cases (Tiskilwa, IL, and Columbus, OH), probable cause has yet to be determined because investigations by the National Transportation Safety Board (NTSB) are ongoing.

Table 1. Recent Railroad Hazmat Accidents

Location	Date
Minot, ND	January 18, 2002
Macdona, TX	June 29, 2004
Graniteville, SC	January 5, 2005
Anding, MS	July 10, 2005
Texarkana, AR	October 15, 2005
New Brighton, PA	October 20, 2006
Shepherdsville, KY	January 16, 2007
Oneida, NY	March 12, 2007
Painesville, OH	October 10, 2007
Cherry Valley, IL	June 19, 2009
Arcadia, OH	February 6, 2011
Tiskilwa, IL	October 17, 2011
Columbus, OH	July 11, 2012

---

[1] Some railroad-hauled hazmat is also carried in covered hopper cars, intermodal containers, and piggyback trailers.

The hazmat accidents listed at the beginning of Table 1 (specifically, Minot, ND; Macdona, TX; and Graniteville, SC) involved releases of toxic inhalation hazard (TIH) materials such as chlorine and anhydrous ammonia. But since the Painesville, OH, accident of October 2007 and the most recent accident in Columbus, OH, in July 2012, general-purpose cars carrying flammable materials such as ethanol have been breached. Moreover, data obtained from the Universal Machine Language Equipment Register (UMLER) in October 2011 indicate that general-purpose tank cars with DOT111 specification represent about two-thirds of the total tank car fleet, whereas pressure cars with DOT105 and DOT112 specifications represent less than one-fifth of the overall population.[2]

Improving the safety of hazmat transportation by rail can be accomplished by investing resources in either the track or the equipment. Track-related improvements include upgrading the infrastructure and mandating more frequent maintenance and inspection programs, whereas equipment improvements entail the development of safety features pertaining to the rolling stock. The focus of this report is on the latter.

In general, accidental loss of hazmat lading from railroad tank cars occurs from four sources: (1) releases from head impacts, (2) releases from shell or side impacts, (3) releases from top fittings, and (4) releases from bottom fittings. Accident statistics collected on tank cars carrying TIH materials suggest that while less than half of all releases are caused by failures in the head and shell, such failures account for 85 percent of the total gallons of lost lading [3]. Tank cars carrying TIH require safety features such as head shields to protect against the threat of a head impact. At the present time, however, a similar design feature to protect the tank against the threat of a shell or side impact has not yet been developed.

This report describes basic research to explore the application of welded steel sandwich panels as a means to provide protection to tank cars in the event of an impacting object striking the shell (i.e., side) of the tank. The research was conducted over a three-year span and was sponsored by the FRA Office of Research and Development. Several organizations made contributions to the research project. The John A. Volpe National Transportation Systems Center (Volpe Center) provided technical support by conducting analytical studies, designing various test series ranging from the component-level to the full-scale impact test, and helping to guide the overall research effort. Cellular Materials International, Inc. (CMI) was under contract with FRA to provide expertise concerning certain aspects of sandwich panels, such as manufacturing development, fabrication processes, and evaluations of material properties. The culmination of the research project was a full-scale shell impact test performed by Transportation Technology Center, Inc. (TTCI) in Pueblo, CO. The full-scale test demonstrated that a 6-foot by 6-foot protective sandwich panel made with 3-inch tubular cores could successfully protect a DOT105J500W specification tank car (filled to 10 percent outage and an internal pressure of 100 psi) against a shell or side impact from a 12-inch by 12-inch indenter mounted on a ram car weighing 295,725 pounds and travelling at a speed of 17.8 miles per hour (mph). Figure 1 shows a schematic of the test setup in which the tank car with the protective panel is positioned against a barrier on one side and struck by the ram car on the other.

---

[2] UMLER data from October 2011 indicates that the North American tank car fleet consisted of a total of 314,561 tank cars, at that time. Of this total population, 212,373 were DOT111 specification cars; 34,474 were DOT112 cars; and 26,087 were DOT105 cars.

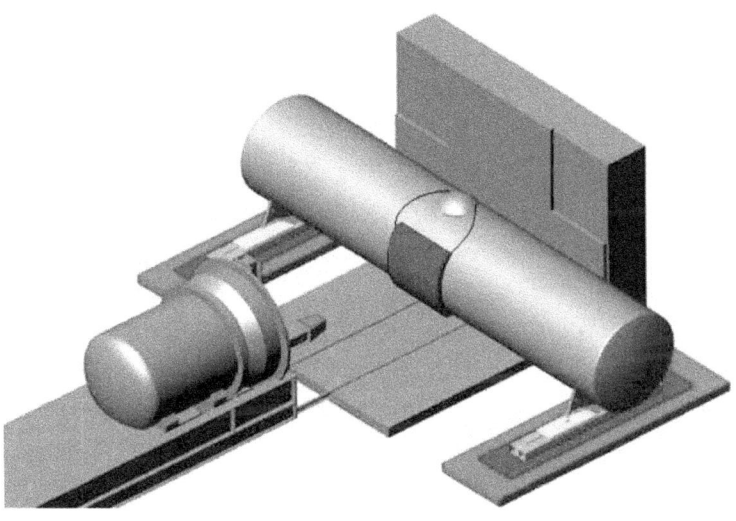

Figure 1. Schematic of Full-Scale Shell Impact Test Setup

Section 1 of this report describes the objectives of the basic research and summarizes the research activities leading up to the conduct of the full-scale shell impact test. In previously performed research activities, component-level testing was conducted to examine the performance of various sandwich panel designs under quasi-static loading conditions, specifically uniaxial compression and three-point bending. Comparisons between these test results and companion analyses were reported previously [4,5]. Moreover, the selection of the sandwich panel design used in the full-scale impact test was based on the results of these component-level tests.

Section 2 of this report discusses manufacturing considerations regarding the construction of welded steel sandwich panels to protect the commodity-carrying tank from an impacting object. Such considerations include the selection of core geometry, selection of material for the core and the face sheets, and welding procedure to build the protective panel. The availability of the materials in certain thicknesses and shapes was a significant factor in the selection process.

Section 3 provides the specific details of the full-scale impact test. This section also includes a description of the selected panel design, material selection, and manufacturing processes. This section also describes a retrofit to modify the indenter that was mounted onto the ram car. A previous full-scale shell impact test that was performed to puncture the commodity-carrying tank used an indenter with a 6-inch by 6-inch footprint. CMI designed the retrofit, which entailed the use of a steel cap reinforced by gussets to cover the existing indenter and create a 12-inch by 12-inch footprint at the impact surface.

Section 4 summarizes the research results. Section 5 discusses the implications of the overall research effort. The potential use of sandwich structures as a retrofit to existing railroads tank cars as a protection system against the threat of shell puncture is considered.

The appendices of this report give detailed information regarding the manufacture of the protective panel that was developed for the full-scale shell impact test. This manufacturing information provided by CMI includes estimates of labor, material, and capital equipment needed to build similar panels. In addition, options for the level of protection, in terms of coverage of the tank shell, are detailed. Finally, concepts or methods to attach the protective panel to existing tank cars are outlined.

1.1 Research Objectives

Over the past several decades, the Government and the railroad industry have sponsored research to improve the safety of railroad tank cars. This research led to the development of thermal protection, double-shelf couplers, large-capacity pressure relief valves, and head shields. In 2007, shortly after the occurrence of a series of train accidents involving the release of TIH materials, research efforts focused on understanding the structural performance of tank cars under accident loading conditions [2]. An objective of this research was to develop more effective strategies for maintaining tank structural integrity under accident loading conditions. The framework used in this research to evaluate potentially improved designs is shown in Figure 2.

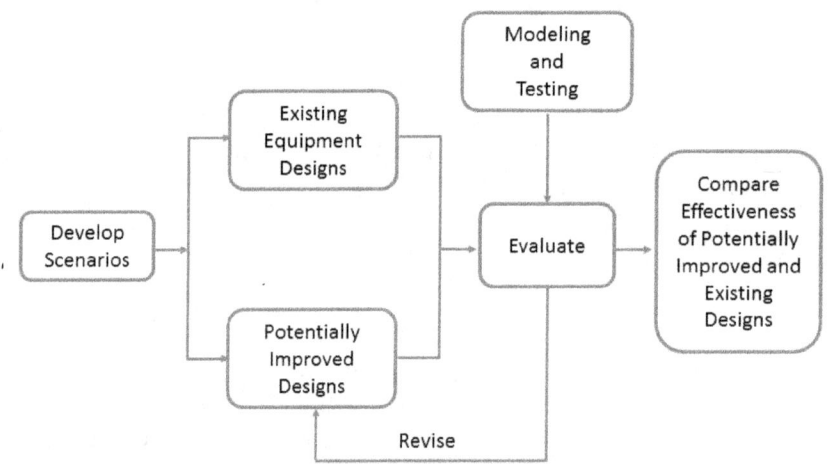

Figure 2. Research Framework

Given the space and weight limitations of existing tank cars, innovative use of materials to develop safety design features was also considered as an objective. One of the technologies identified to improve the puncture resistance of tank cars is the engineered metal sandwich structure [6]. Engineered metal sandwich structures offer several characteristics that appeared attractive for the purpose of increasing the puncture resistance of tank cars. The engineered metal sandwich structure can be fabricated in a variety of core geometries and from a variety of materials. Because sandwich structures can be made of commercial, off-the-shelf metal sheets and structural shapes, a wide variety of geometries are achievable using similar fabrication techniques. Additionally, sandwich structures were thought to offer the potential to be constructed with a rounded (nonplanar) form that would conform to the side of the tank shell.

1.2   Sandwich Panels

Sandwich structures are generally composed of two face sheets separated by a geometric core. In the traditional design of sandwich structures, the separation of the face sheets by the core increases the area moment of inertia of the panel, which produces a higher bending stiffness-to-weight ratio than solid or monolithic plates containing the same volume of metal. The face sheets carry almost all of the bending and in-plane loads while the core carries the shear load to prevent the face sheets from sliding past one another. Although sandwich panels may be fabricated from a variety of materials, steel panels were considered in this research program. This program focused on readily-available materials (e.g. off-the-shelf metal sheets and tubes) that offered a high degree of manufacturability. An exemplar sandwich panel featuring tubular cores is shown in Figure 3.

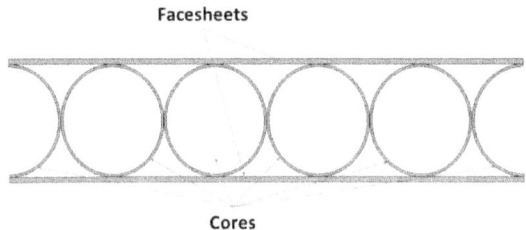

Figure 3. Sandwich Panel with Components Identified

In the event of a collision or impact scenario, welded steel sandwich panels provide puncture protection to the commodity-carrying tank through load blunting and energy absorption. Blunting means that the impact load is distributed over a larger area of the tank with respect to the indenter footprint, effectively increasing the energy needed to puncture the tank. Protective panels also work to absorb the collision energy. By absorbing energy in an external structure, the energy demands placed on the tank shell are reduced. Indeed, the load-blunting and energy-absorption capabilities of sandwich panels depend on the core shape or geometry, as well as the materials used for the panel.

1.3   Previous Test Series

The remainder of this section summarizes testing related to shell puncture protection conducted prior to the full-scale impact test of the tank car equipped with a protective panel. Figure 4 compares the previous tests with the full-scale impact test with the protective panel. The previous tests are categorized in the figure as full-scale shell impact tests on tank cars designed to carry liquid chlorine, a TIH material, and component-level, quasi-static tests on flat sandwich panels. The full-scale tests provided technical information on the structural behavior of tank cars under shell impact loading. Results and analyses of the previous full-scale impact tests have been described previously [14]. The component-level tests generated technical information on the deformation behavior of sandwich panels under specific and controlled loading conditions. In each of these previous tests, the research framework shown in Figure 2 was followed to confirm, verify, and validate analytical results and establish confidence and credibility in the modeling activities.

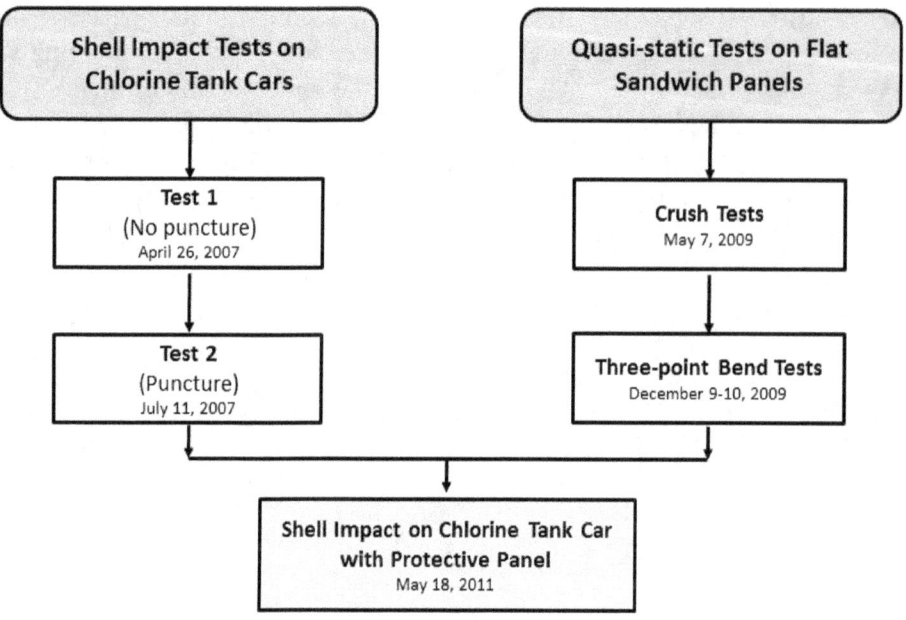

Figure 4. Confluence of Full-Scale and Component Level Tests

1.3.1 Preproduction Compression Testing at CMI

CMI manufactured and tested a series of panels to develop cost-effective manufacturing techniques and to provide data to assist in selecting panel designs for testing. Examples of the preproduction panels are outlined below. Larger samples were manufactured to identify suitable manufacturing practices for various core configurations. The smaller compression samples were tested using a 250-kip compression tester.

2-foot by 2-foot panels

A set of 2-foot by 2-foot panels with X-cores, tubular cores, and square tube cores with variations in thickness were manufactured. The goal of this exercise was to establish manufacturing methods to produce robust performance for each core topology. The various welding processes studied included resistance spot welding, gas metal arc welding – pulsed spray transfer mode (GMAW-P), and plasma welding. To reduce the heat affected area, and hence the distortion, intermittent plug or GMAW-P welding was studied in detail.

Small Test Panels

The compression testing was conducted on a series of 4-inch by 4-inch panels with ¼-inch Domex face sheets and 2-inch diameter ⅛-inch wall thickness 1010 pipe. For comparison, panels with 2.875-inch by 7.86-inch long square tubes were fabricated and crushed. Each of the panels was welded differently to develop fabrication techniques and characterize the effect of welding geometries on panel performance. The panels were compression tested using a 250-kip compression tester at the Virginia Transportation Research Council (VTRC) facility in Charlottesville. Data, including force and displacement, were collected for the first 1 inch of displacement. However, the panels were crushed beyond 1 inch.

One of the key outcomes of this prefabrication study was that it provided insight into the crushing behavior of the panels. The crushing behavior of the round tube cores is very different from the square tube cores. The contrast is structural response is shown in Figure 5. The square tube oriented to form a diamond core exhibits a comparatively high initial strength, but once failure occurs, the panel loses all strength. Figure 6 illustrates how the diamond core crushes nonuniformly. In comparison, when the sandwich panels with round tubes crush, there is an initial steep rise in load followed by a gradual plateau. Following this plateau, the core exhibits a steep rise in load. Once it reaches the peak load, the core collapses and the force drops. When the load is first applied, the tubes are squeezed at the top and bottom and move outward. As the tube is forced outward, it meets with resistance from the adjacent tubes. As a result, the round tubes begin to square off (see Figure 7). The first threshold is the load at which the round tubes take a square cross section. Once the tubes can no longer move outward, the load increases as the squared tubes begin to crush. The second plateau is the load at which the squared tubes begin to collapse.

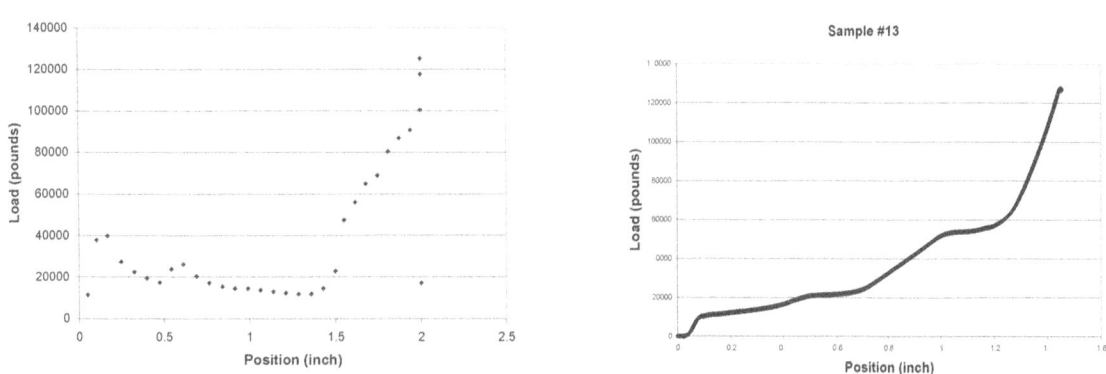

Figure 5. Load versus Position for Diamond Panel (Left) and Round-Tube Panel (Right)

Figure 6. Photos of Diamond Panel during Crushing

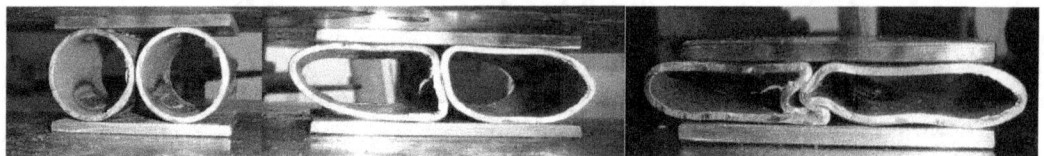

Figure 7. Photos of Round-Tube Panel during Crushing

The following observations were made from the preproduction compression testing of the small sandwich panel samples:

- Round tube cores have a different crushing behavior than square tubes or X-core.
- Testing speed did not affect panel compression behavior within the limits investigated.
- The load to crush a panel with the face sheets plug welded to the core was greater than the load needed to crush a panel in which the core was welded together but the face sheets were not welded to the core.
- When the pipes were stitched welded together, the load versus displacement response was more linear and there were not two thresholds.
- If not constrained, the cores will move laterally during compression.

To prevent lateral movement of the round tubes, it was recommended that two half tubes be welded on each end of the panel such that a panel with five tubes would have four tubes in the center and a tube cut in half lengthwise on each end, as shown in Figure 8.

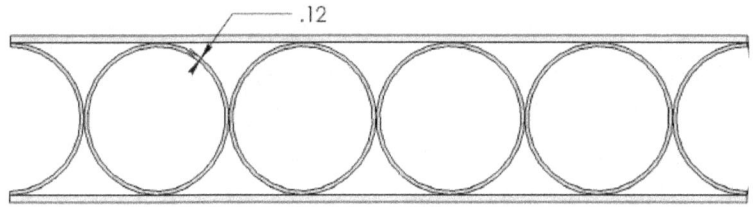

Figure 8. Drawing of Recommended Round Tube Core Design to Prevent Lateral Movement

4.5-inch by 9-inch Panels

Compression tests were performed on 4.5-inch by 9-inch samples using 3-inch OD tube with various welding geometries. The face sheets were ¼-inch Domex and the tube used, due to its availability, was 4130. The deformation patterns of the samples with the tubes with and without welds between them were almost identical; however, the compression data indicated that the sample made with the tubes welded together was significantly stronger. Regardless of whether the tubes were welded together or not, the 4130 tubes fractured at the bend lines (see Figure 9). In previous tests, 1010 tubes of the same dimension bent but did not crack in compression. Although 1010 tubes had a lower tensile strength than the 4130 tubes, the cores with 1010 tubes exhibited a greater crush resistance (i.e., the force to crush the panel a given distance was greater). Based on these and follow-up analyses, and due to the difficulty of welding 4130, 1010 steel was selected as the core material for the test panels.

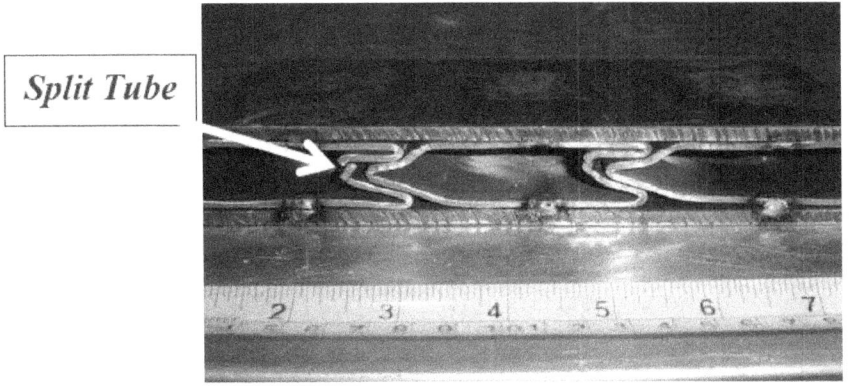

Figure 9. 3-Inch 4130 Pipe Sample with Tubes Welded Together

1.3.2 Uniaxial Compression Testing at ATLSS

Using the information obtained from the panel prefabrication study and test data, as well as Volpe's finite element analysis on selected designs, fourteen panels were selected for testing under uniaxial compression at Lehigh University's Fritz Engineering Lab. The objective of the tests was to measure the force versus displacement behavior of the sandwich panels when subjected to uniform loading on the face sheet. Because the top and bottom face sheets were loaded uniformly, the test results reflect the core compression behavior. These tests were employed to determine the mode of crushing for the various core types and to compare manufacturing techniques.

Core Designs and Manufacturing

All fourteen panels were manufactured by CMI and tested at Lehigh University. Three core designs were selected for panel fabrication: round tube core, X-core, and diamond core (i.e., square tube rotated 45 degrees). The specifics (materials, weld types, sizes) of the eight designs used for these panels are shown in Table 2. Two panels of the P1, P2, P3, P4, X1, and X2 designs were manufactured. One of each set of panels was manually welded and the second one in each set was robotically welded. To examine variation in fabrication, the 6-inch by 24-inch diamond core test articles (D1 and D2) were manufactured with and without stitch welds. However, one panel (D2) has the core elements welded together and the other (D1) does not. All core to core welds were done manually for the diamond panel and the 2-inch round tube panel. The welding parameters are shown in Table 3. Photos of some of the manufactured panels are shown in Figure 10. Note that there was no post heat treatment done to the panels after panel manufacturing. The weld procedures and the material used do not require such treatments.

Table 2. Panel Details for Quasi-Static Compression Tests

	P1	P2	P3	P4	X1	X2	D1	D2
Panel Number	0047-01 0047-02	0047-03 0047-04	0047-05 0047-06	0047-07 0047-08	0047-09 0047-10	0047-11 0047-12	0047-13	0047-14
Core	Round Tube	Round Tube	Round Tube	Round Tube	X-Core	X-Core	Diamond	Diamond
Face sheet thickness	0.25"	0.25"	0.25"	0 25"	0.25"	0.25"	0.25"	0.25"
Face sheet material	100XF	100XF	100XF	100XF	100XF	100XF	100XF	100XF
Core Height	5"	3"	2"	2"	5"	5"	2.62"	2.62"
Core Thickness	0.125"	0.125"	0.125"	0.125"	0.125"	0.125"	0.125"	0.125"
Core Density	7.8%	12.5%	18%	18%	7%	7%	13%	13%
Core Material	1010	1010	1010	1010	1010	1010	1010	1010
Panel Width	5 cores 25"	8 cores 24"	12 cores 24"	12 cores 24"	5 hats 27"	5 hats 27"	9 cores 24"	9 cores 24"
Panel Depth	6"	6"	6"	6"	6"	6"	6"	6"
Weld Type	Slot/Skip	Slot/Skip	Slot/Skip	Slot/Skip & Stitch b/n core elements	Spot	Slot and Spot	Slot and Skip	Slot/Skip and Stitch b/n core elements
No. of panels	2	2	2	2	2	2	1	1
Manufacturing Comments	3/8"x 1" slots; 2 welds/core per side; 1 panel manually and 1 panel robotically welded	3/8"x 1" slots; 2 welds/core per side; 1 panel manually and 1 panel robotically welded	3/8"x 1" slots; 2 welds/core per side; 1 panel manually and 1 panel robotically welded	3/8"x 1" slots; 2 welds/core per side; 1 panel manually and 1 panel robotically welded; ¼"x1" stitch welds b/n core elements	3/8" RSW speed 4" apart for core and face sheet welds	3/8"x 1" slots; 2 welds/core per side; 3/8" RSW spaced 4" apart for core welds; 1 panel manually and 1 panel robotically welded	3/8"x 1" slots; 2 welds/core per side; robotically welded	3/8"x 1" slots; 2 welds/core per side; ¼"x 1" stitch welds b/n core elements; robotically welded

Table 3. GMAW-P Welding Parameters

Process	Volts	Amps
Robotic	16	150
Manual	20	130
Filler Wire	ER70S-3	
Gas	92% Argon/8% CO_2	

6"x2'x5" Pipe Round Tube Core Test Article (P1)

6"x2'x3" Round Tube Core Test Article (P2)

6"x2'x2" Round Tube Core Test Article (P3)

6"x2' X-Core Shell Test Article (X1)

6"x2' Diamond Core Test Article (D2)

Figure 10. Photos of Manufactured Panels for Uniaxial Compression Tests

Observations

The panels were placed on a flat block in a 5,000-kip Baldwin compression testing machine at Lehigh University's Fritz Engineering Laboratory. A movable test head was positioned slightly above the block at the top of the panel and moved down at 0.2 inch per minute. This speed was selected to determine quasi-static material deformation behavior avoiding any strain rate effects. The displacement of the top plate was measured by two string potentiometers mounted between the fixed and moveable heads of the universal testing machine. Each panel was compressed to approximately 50 percent of its original height. The applied load was recorded and two video cameras documented the tests in progress.

Load versus displacement curves for two sandwich panels subjected to uniform uniaxial compression are shown in Figure 11. The peak or maximum load is considered the crushing load. The crushing load for the panel with the 2-inch round-tube core is 615 kips. The crushing load for the panel with the diamond core is 398 kips, or about 35 percent lower than the crushing load for the round-tube core panel.

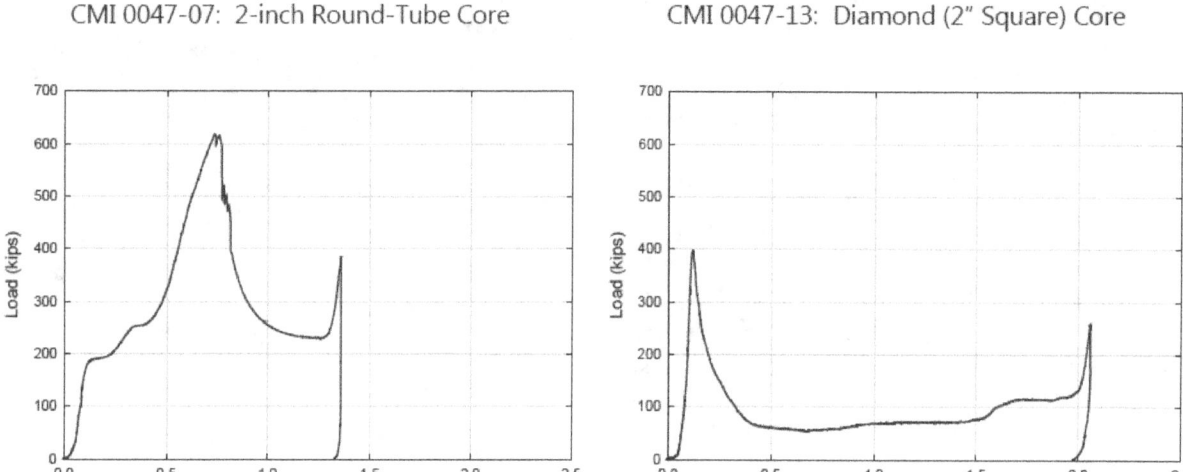

CMI 0047-07: 2-inch Round-Tube Core   CMI 0047-13: Diamond (2″ Square) Core

Figure 11. Load versus Displacement Curves for Round-Tube and Diamond Core Panels

The following observations were made from these uniaxial compression test series:
- Each core (i.e. round tube, diamond, and X-core) exhibited a different characteristic crushing behavior.
- The load-displacement results for the round tube and diamond core geometry were repeatable between samples.
- The X-core panels had the lowest repeatability in terms of load versus displacement behavior and crushed shape. The variability may be due to failures in welds in the X-core panels.
- The X-core samples with spot welding exhibited the lowest crush load.
- The round tubes contacted each other immediately upon crushing and began to deform plastically into a square cross-section.
- For the round-tube core panels, the load to crush the 2-inch round-tube cores was greater than the load to crush the 3-inch tube or 5-inch tube core.
- Because the tube thickness was the same for all panels, the 2-inch tube core panel had the highest core density.
- For most cores, the friction between the support blocks in testing prevented lateral movement of the core. However, the load to crush the 2-inch round tube core was sufficient to overcome this friction and the tubes shifted laterally.

1.3.3 Three-point Bend Testing at ATLSS
The second set of component tests performed in this program was a three-point bend test where the loading would cause large deformation of the face sheet and not solely crush the cores. For

14

this set of tests, the X-core and 5-inch round tube core were eliminated from the test protocol due primarily to their relatively low crush force once the initial peak was overcome. The 2-inch round tube core was eliminated due to the amount of welding necessary to assemble the panel and the difficulty in predicting the lateral shift of the 2-inch round tubes during compression. Based on their performance under uniaxial compression and on their manufacturability, core geometries selected to be included in three-point bend testing were the 3-inch round tube core and the 2-inch square diamond core.

A total of sixteen panels, 18 inches deep by 48 inches wide, were manufactured and tested. The manufacturing and design variables of the panels included the core type (round or square), solid or strip face sheets, manual or robotic welding, and orientation of core elements with respect to supports. Eight panels were constructed using the conventional solid top and bottom face sheets. Six panels were manufactured using strips instead of solid face sheets in an effort to prevent propagation of a crack along the perimeter of an impacting object. Such a crack would allow the impacting object to tear through the panel without engaging the panel's structure outside of the impact area. Two panels were built using a solid face sheet on one side and a face sheet consisting of strips on the other. The test panel cores were either 0.125-inch wall 3-inch OD 1010 steel round tubes or 0.125-inch wall 2-inch OD square tubes. Each square tube was rotated 45 degrees to create a diamond core configuration. In all panels, the face sheets were 0.118-inch 100XF steel. The orientation of the cores was either in the long 48-inch direction or the shorter 18-inch short direction. If the panel had a strip face sheet, the strips would be perpendicular to the length of the core elements. Panels constructed with tubes oriented in the 18-inch short direction were placed in the test fixture with the cores parallel to the test supports, as depicted in Figure 13. The panels with core oriented in the 48-inch longitudinal direction were positioned in the test fixture with tubes perpendicular to the supports. The design specifics of the panels are provided in Table 4.

The strip and solid face sheets were plug welded to the cores using ⅜-inch by 1-inch plug welds. The strips were 3 in wide and had 3-inch spacing between them. The welds were spaced at 6-inch intervals along the core elements for all panels. The weld spacing normal to the core elements was 3 inches for the pipe core elements and 2.67 inches for the diamond core elements. Figure 12 shows photographs of panels with the strip face sheets and with the solid face sheets.

Table 4. Panel Details for Three-Point Bend Tests

Serial Number	Core	Core Orientation Relative to Supports	Face Sheet Type	Weld Type	Weight (lb)
0047-19	Round Tube	Parallel	Solid	Manual	139.5
0047-15	Diamond	Parallel	Solid	Manual	139.5
0047-26	Round Tube	Parallel	Strip	Robotic	111.0
0047-24	Diamond	Parallel	Strip	Robotic	111.5
0047-21	Round Tube	Perpendicular	Solid	Manual	141.0
0047-17	Diamond	Perpendicular	Solid	Manual	140.0
0047-25	Round Tube	Perpendicular	Strip	Robotic	110.5
0047-23	Diamond	Perpendicular	Strip	Robotic	109.5
0047-29	Diamond	Perpendicular	Solid & Strip	Manual	126.0
0047-20	Round Tube	Parallel	Solid	Robotic	139.5
0047-16	Diamond	Parallel	Solid	Robotic	139.5
0047-28	Diamond	Parallel	Strip	Manual	109.0
0047-22	Round Tube	Perpendicular	Solid	Robotic	142.5
0047-18	Diamond	Perpendicular	Solid	Robotic	137.0
0047-27	Diamond	Perpendicular	Strip	Manual	110.0
0047-30	Diamond	Perpendicular	Solid & Strip	Manual	126.0

Strip Face Sheets

Solid Face Sheets

Figure 12. Photos of Panels for Three-Point Bend Testing

The three-point bend tests were conducted on the Baldwin compression tester at Lehigh University, which was used in the previous test series. In order to apply the bending load, CMI designed and manufactured a fixture and load application block to accommodate the panels in the testing machine, as shown in Figure 13. The fixture consisted of two 4-inch round solid bars which were welded parallel to each other with 24-inch center-to-center spacing. The round bars were welded to a 1-inch plate supported by small pieces of steel that acted to resist deflection of the round bars during the compression tests. This fixture was placed on the bottom platen of the compression tester and each panel was centered on top of the two 4-inch bars.

16

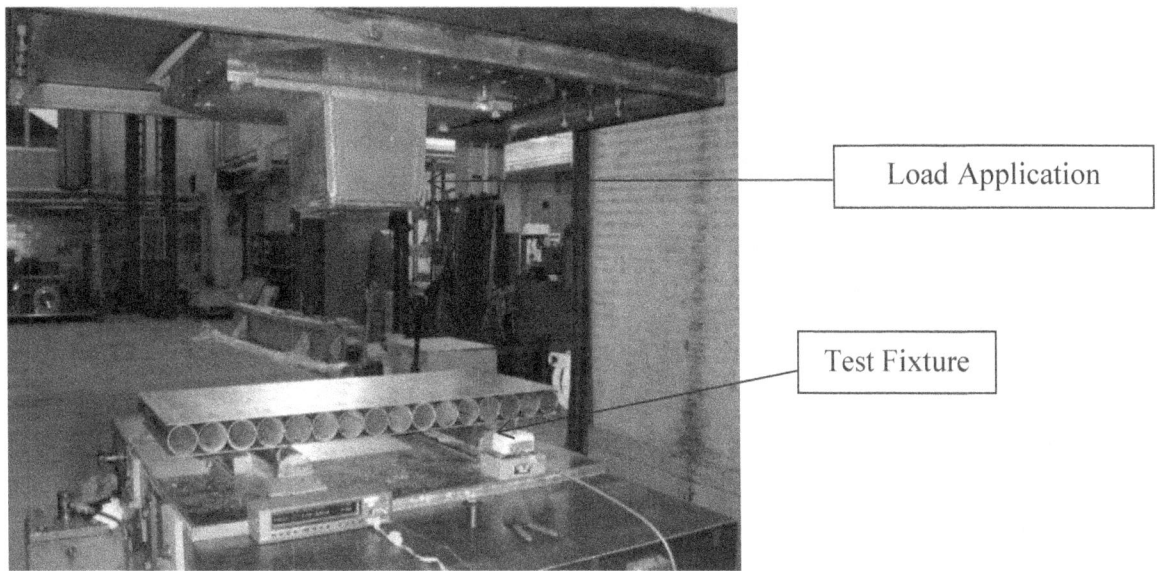

Figure 13. Photo of Panel in Three-Point Bend Setup

An approximate cubic steel load application block was manufactured by welding together 1-inch steel plates. It was machined to have a 12-inch by 12-inch contact area with 1-inch radius corners. The block was tapered to a 13-inch width at the top to facilitate removal of the block from the panels after testing. The load application block was centered over the panel and was attached to a 1-inch plate that was in turn bolted to the top platen of the compression tester.

The initial test protocol was to bend and deform the panels with the ram traveling at 0.25 inch per minute until the top face sheet moved downward approximately 3 in or until it reached the top of the 4-inch diameter round bars of the bottom fixture. At Lehigh, the test protocol was modified so that the ram traveled approximately 6 inches until the panels were deformed almost completely, with the load application block nearly in contact with the bottom test fixture. Changing the protocol to cause more severe deformation allowed observation of the crush behavior to a completely flat state.

Figure 14 shows the bending behavior of panel number 0047-20, which has solid face sheets and pipes parallel to the supports. The corresponding load displacement curve is also shown in the figure. Figure 15 shows the bending behavior of panel number 0047-21, which also has solid face sheets, but in this case the pipes are perpendicular to the supports. Figure 16 illustrates the bending behavior of panel number 0047-17, which has solid face sheets and diamond core perpendicular to the supports. In some tests, bubble wrap was placed under the panel, as shown in Figure 17, in order to estimate the area over which the load was transferred. Although the indenter was 12-inch by 12-inch, the bubble wrap indicated that the load was distributed over a larger area.

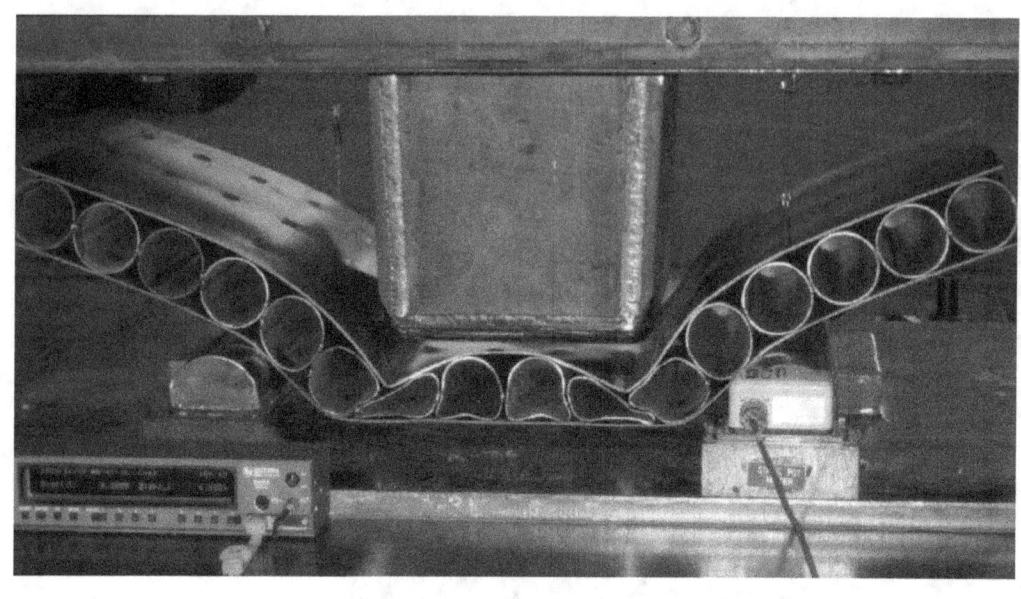

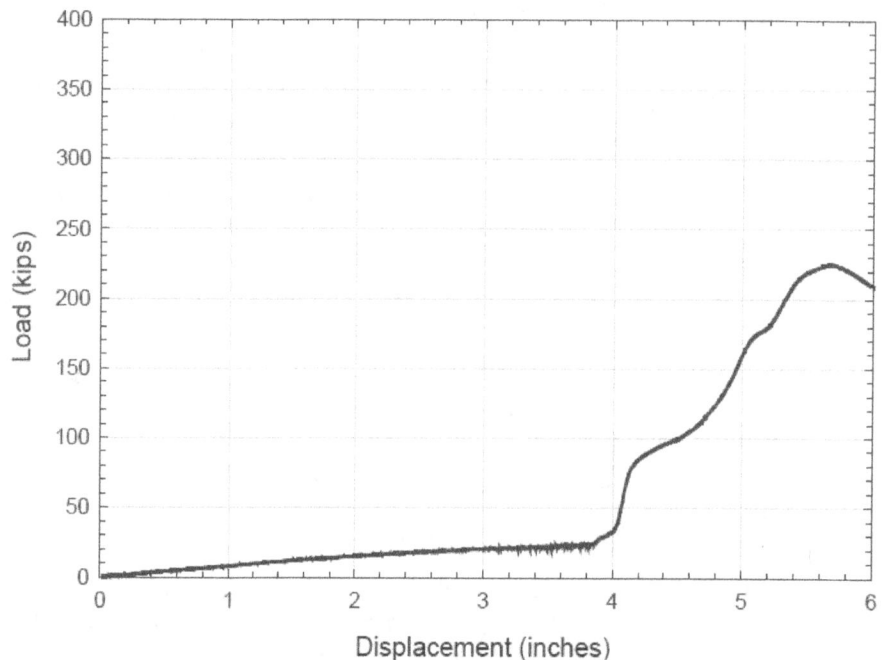

Figure 14. Deformation of Panel No. 0047-20 and Corresponding Load-Displacement Curve

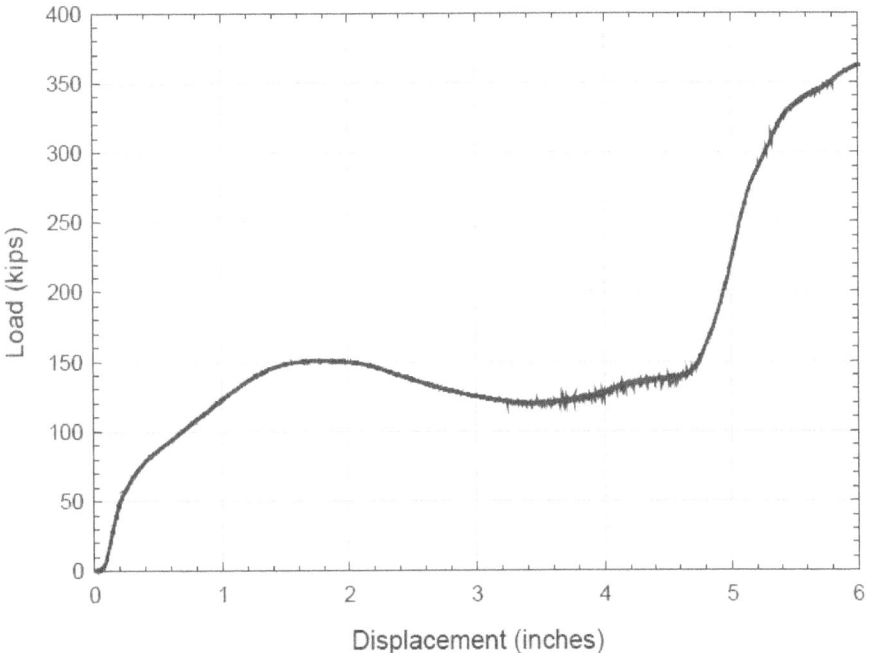

Figure 15. Deformation of Panel No. 0047-21 and Corresponding Load-Displacement Curve

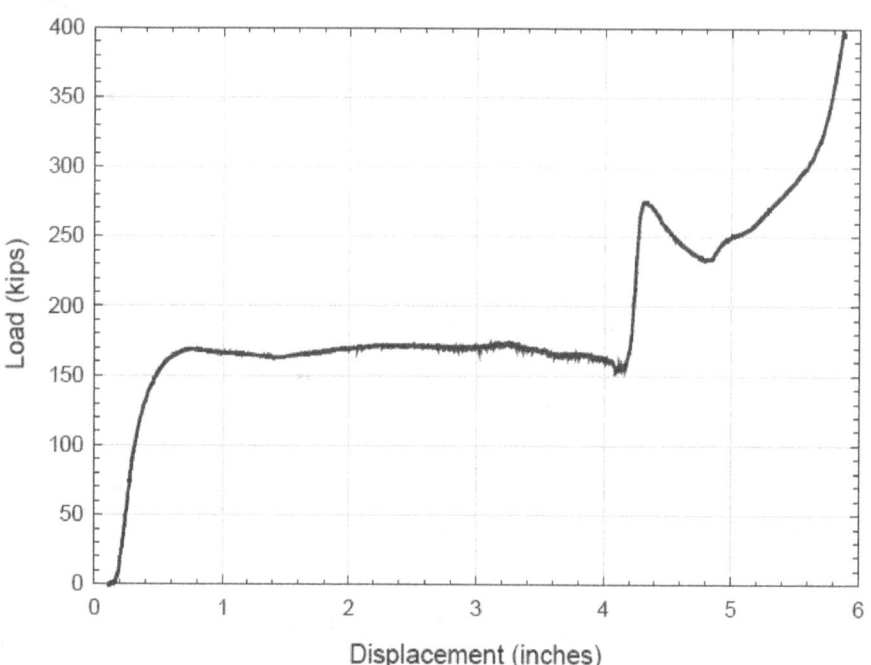

Figure 16. Deformation of Panel No. 0047-17 and Corresponding Load-Displacement Curve

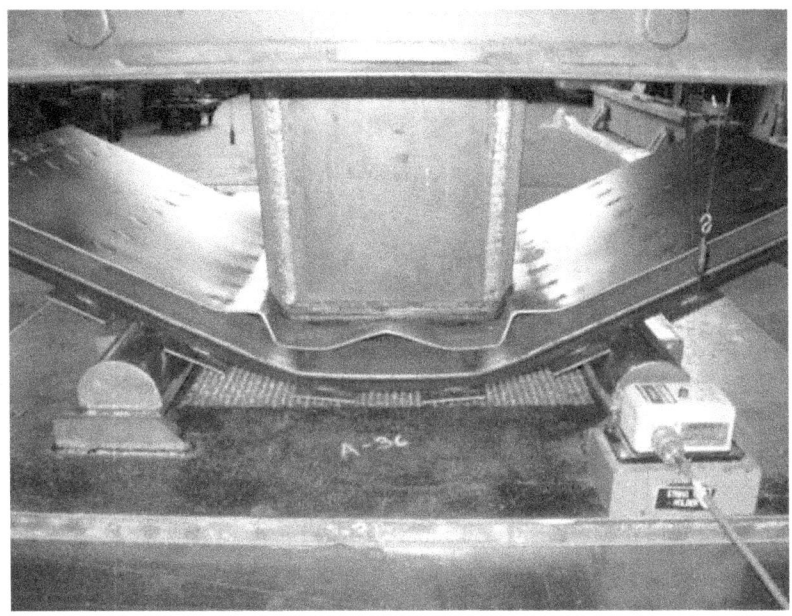

Figure 17. Panel in Three-Point Bend Test with Bubble Wrap to Estimate Load Transfer Area

The following observations were made from the three-point bend tests:
- Panels with the core perpendicular to the supports require more force to deform than panels with the core oriented parallel to the supports.
- When the core elements are parallel to the supports, the elements are able to move past each other so that only the face sheet provides initial bending strength.
- Panels with solid face sheets are stiffer than similar panels with strip face sheets. The panels with solid face sheets require a greater force to deform.
- The strip face sheets did not crack in the diamond core panels with perpendicular orientation, but the solid face sheets did.
- Localized crushing of the pipe cores was observed in three locations: under the load application block and above each of the two supports, whereas localized crushing of the diamond cores was observed only under the load application block.
- The loaded area, as measured by the bubble wrap test, was approximately 50 percent greater than the 12-inch by 12-inch surface area of the indenter.

2.   Manufacturing Considerations

FRA awarded a Small Business Innovation Research (SBIR) contract to CMI to design and manufacture test articles for the research project. CMI's experience in fabricating steel sandwich structures and developing manufacturing plans for other platforms was applied to develop economical manufacturing processes and welding techniques for railroad tank car application.

2.1   Materials

The typical steel used for the tank car construction is TC128-B steel. This steel is not manufactured in the thin gauges needed for sandwich construction. In addition, TC128-B requires a stress relieving treatment after welding. Therefore, CMI considered alternative steels for the protective panels. The objective was to locate a commercially available steel composition that has high tensile strength (around 100 ksi) and ductility around 30 percent in terms of linear elongation. High strength low alloy (HSLA) steels provide increased strength over conventional carbon steels; therefore, this group of steels was considered. HSLA steels are identified by their mechanical properties, not composition. Because they are much stronger and tougher than ordinary carbon steels, they are typically used in applications such as car and truck fabrication, bridge design, street lighting poles, oil storage tanks, and earth moving equipment where strength-to-weight ratio is important. These steels are typically highly formable and weldable and are resistant to corrosion, which is important for long-term use. The mechanical properties of the HSLA steels considered and other steels that surfaced as a result of this investigation are listed in Table 5.

Table 5. Minimum Mechanical Properties of Steels Considered
(All values are minimum except where the ranges were provided by the manufacturer)

	Tensile Strength (ksi)	Yield Strength (ksi)	Elongation (%)	Typical Applications
AISI 4130 [7]	81	52	28	Structural and aircraft tubing, bicycle frames, clutch and flywheel components, roll cages
AISI 1010 [8]	52	44	20	Structural and vehicle components including body, fender, pans, washers, rivets, brushings, and nails
Modified 1010* [9]	72.1	61.7	38	
HSLA50 [10]	60	50	20	Truck frames, brackets, crane booms, rail cars, ship construction, towers
Domex 100XF [11]	110	100	15	Trailers, construction and agricultural equipment, crane booms, vehicle frames and chassis
TC128-B [12]	81 – 101	50	19 -22	Railroad tank cars
Boron Steel* [13]	214	169	5-6	Vehicles

* Not readily available in tubes required for program

The 100XF HSLA material is far superior in strength compared with TC128-B and does not need to be stress relieved subsequent to welding. Therefore, CMI investigated this steel for the protection panels. Because various core geometries were being considered in this research program, one consideration during material selection was the availability of different tubular forms made of the same material. Although HSLA 100XF grades are available in flat sheet and tubular form, the tubular forms in the size ranges of interest could not be located at any vendor, nor through other channels, including major steel mills. The modified 1010 steel is also not available commercially. The standard AISI 1010 steel composition is readily available in all tubular shapes of interest to our program. Accordingly, this material was selected as the core material for the initial compression tests. AISI 4130 was also utilized as the core material for initial compression testing due to its availability. However, the 4130 chrome-moly pipe is difficult to weld. It requires preheat prior to welding and has a propensity for developing weld cracks and a weak heat affected zone (HAZ), both of which result in low fatigue resistance. The higher carbon content and martensitic structure of this metal are contributing factors to its poor weld ability. As a result, this material was not considered for this study. The Domex 100 XF was selected for face sheet material.

Thielsch Engineering performed mechanical testing of the as received tubes and face sheets. The average mechanical properties, with standard deviation in parentheses, of five samples of each material are summarized in Table 6. The minimum values for 1010 steel are 44 ksi for yield strength, 52 ksi for tensile strength, and 20 percent for elongation.

Table 6. Average Mechanical Properties of as Received Tubes and Face Sheets

Material	Ultimate Tensile Strength (ksi)	Yield Strength, 0.2% offset (ksi)	Elongation in 1 inch (%)
5" diameter x 0.125" wall x 6" long 4130 Steel Round Pipe	118 (1.4)	97.5 (2.5)	17.8 (0.45)
5" diameter x 0.125" wall x 6" long 1010 Steel Round Pipe	52 (0.27)	37 (1.2)	38.7 (0.91)
3" diameter x 0.125" wall x 6" long 1010 Steel Round Pipe	54 (0.42)	43 (0.6)	35.1 (1.3)
2" diameter x 0.125" wall x 6" long 1010 Steel Round Pipe	63 (0.42)	52 (1.3)	32.3 (0.45)
2" diameter x 0.125" wall x 6" long 1010 Steel Square Pipe	71 (0.96)	60.5 (2.0)	21.9 (0.42)
1/4" x 8" x 10 Domex Plate	113 (0.84)	101 (1.1)	17.8* (0.27)

Note: All ductile failures
* Elongation in 2 inches

Examination of the measured data shows significant variation in mechanical properties among the samples tested from the same 1010 steel grade. This can be attributed to the manufacturing process used for each batch of steel from which the specific tubes were produced. Each tube diameter is produced from a different batch of steel which may respond to subsequent mechanical working differently. The final strength of the material depends on the mechanical work experienced by each batch of steel prior to tube welding *and* the amount of post cold drawing done after tube welding. The tubes used for this study are welded and then cold drawn.

2.2 Welding

Many different welding methods were considered for fabricating the panels. The criteria for selecting a welding method were as follows: strength of the weld, distortion (determined by heat input), maximum gap, processing time, equipment cost, post processing, and ability to automate the process. CMI worked with Edison Welding Institute (EWI) to analyze different welding processes. A summary of the processes considered is shown in Table 7.

Table 7. Summary of Different Welding Methods

	Plasma Key Hole Weld w/ Cold Wire	2 Wire Tandem GMAW	Plasma GMAW	Laser/G MAW	GMAW-P Plug Weld	Resistance Spot/Double
Process Speed – in/min	20–30	100–160	20–30	150–200	N/A	2 welds/10 Sec
Equipment Cost	$40K	$40K	$50K	$1,000K	$10K	$35K
Preprocessing	Need a slot				Need a hole	
Maximum Gap	Very Small	Better	Better	Better	Better	None
Can It Be Mechanized?	Yes	Yes	Yes	Yes	Yes	Yes
Distortion (Heat Input kJ/in)	40–50	25	40–50	10–15	Local	Low

Plasma welding, laser welding, Gas Metal Arc Welding (GMAW), Pulsed GMAW-P, Resistance Spot Welding, and hybrid welding techniques that employ a combination of weld practices are among the processes that appeared amenable to welding thin-gauge materials incorporating various automation methods. Both plasma welding and plasma/GMAW hybrid welding processes generate intense heat input leading to higher heat distortion. Laser/GMAW, which is superior to all the other processes considered, is highly sophisticated and not readily available for routine manufacturing. The upfront equipment costs are very high compared with other processes considered herein. The GMAW welding process is a widely used welding method. Several advances have been made to improve this process in recent years. The heat input for this process can be controlled by the welding method used. One preferred method to minimize and precisely control the heat input without compromising weld efficiency is to pulse the arc. This process coupled with plug welding, GMAW-P, in contrast to a continuous weld, is expected to create minimum distortion and lower cost. This process can be readily adopted with minimum investment. The resistance spot welding process is another weld process that is widely used for very thin gauge materials and is being adopted for moderate thickness material. Both the GMAW-P and resistance spot welding equipment were available in house. Therefore, these two processes were selected for initial weld trials.

Several test welds were made using GMAW-P plug welding and resistance spot welding. Both flat plate-to-plate and flat plate-to-pipe welds were evaluated. A 0.25-inch Domex plate was welded to either 0.118-inch Domex flat plate or 1010 steel pipe with similar wall thickness.

Tensile tests were conducted on both the plate-to-plate and plate-to-pipe assembly that had been welded with these two processes. Both single and double plug welds, spaced 1 inch apart, were tested in plate-to-plate and plate-to-pipe combination. Duplicate samples were welded using resistance spot welding. All the weld samples were tested at CMI. The plug weld samples failed outside the weld with the exception of the single plug weld to the plate, which sheared in the weld. The single plug welds to pipe actually pulled material out of the pipe such that failure occurred in the 1010 pipe. One such failure is shown in Figure 18. The double plug weld to pipe forced the failure to occur in the Domex plate (see Figure 18). However, the strength of the weld was not as high as the plate-to-plate weld.

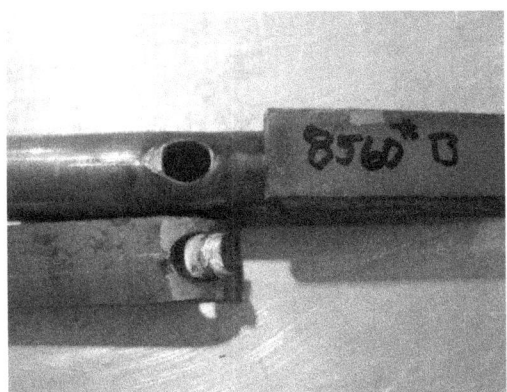

Figure 18. Single (Left) and Double (Right) GMAW-P Plug Welds to 1-Inch Pipe

Subsequently, samples with different plug weld configurations were tested to identify differences in weld strength based on plug hole geometry. Two ¼-inch Domex plates were welded together using a resistance spot weld and Pulsed Gas Metal Arc Welding (GMAW-P) plug welds with various geometries. The average results of two tensile tests for each weld technique and geometry are shown in Figure 19. As was expected, due to its overall larger weld area, the ½-inch by 1½-inch plug weld exhibited the greatest strength. However, if the load per square inch of weld is compared rather than total load, the ½-inch round plug welds exhibited superior strength.

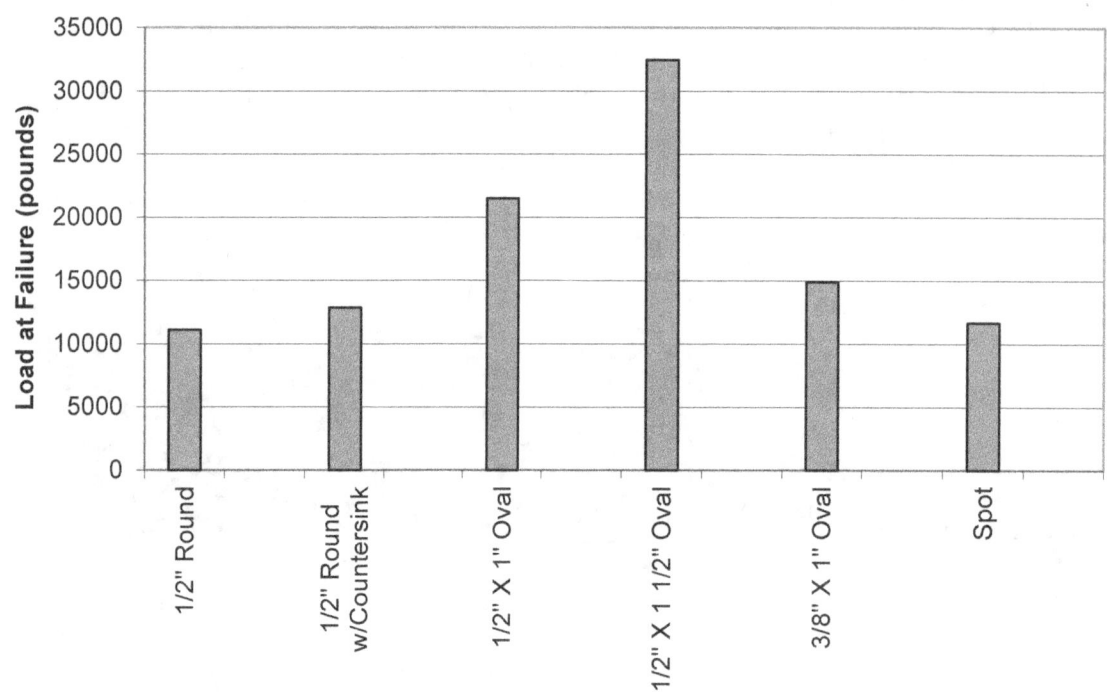

Figure 19. Average Load at Failure for Various Welds

The total processing time, including preparation and welding times, was estimated for each weld configuration. Although resistance spot welding appeared to be the most cost effective method, technical issues precluded it from being a viable candidate; therefore, GMAW-P plug welding was down-selected to manufacture the panels. The optimal weld spacing between plug welds was then investigated. Tensile tests on Domex strips were conducted for various plug sizes and spacing and the average loads at failure for two samples of each configuration are shown in Figure 20. In these tests, the top plate was 0.25 inch and the bottom plate was 0.118 inch. Both plates were 4 inches wide and 18 inches long.

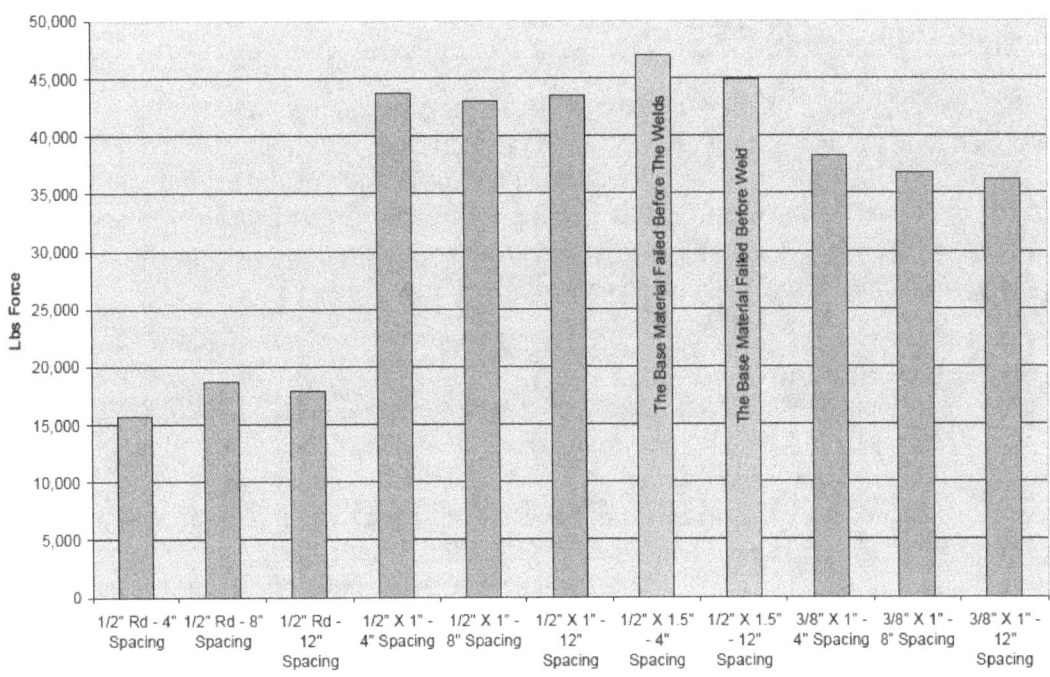

Figure 20. Load to Failure for Various Weld Configurations at 4-Inch, 8-Inch and 12-Inch Spacing

The spacing between welds in the range of 4 to 12 inches had little effect on the total load to failure for any of the weld configurations. Welds spaced greater than 12 inches apart will not provide enough support for the face sheet in the event of an impact from an object with a small area but large amount of kinetic energy. Although the ½-inch by 1½-inch plug welds were the strongest weld, the round tubes do not have sufficient area in contact with the face sheet to accommodate a ½-inch wide weld. Therefore, ⅜-inch by 1½-inch plug welds spaced 8 inches apart on a core element were the down-selected welding procedure for the final panels.

27

3. Full-Scale Impact Testing at TTC

One curved protective panel manufactured by CMI was installed on the shell of a decommissioned tank car and impact tested at the Transportation Technology Center (TTC) located in Pueblo, CO. This section describes (1) the approach and objectives of the full-scale test, (2) details of the protective panel including material selection and manufacturing processes, (3) a retrofit of the indenter to accommodate a larger impact footprint, (4) details of the test setup including instrumentation, and (5) test results and observations.

3.1 Overall Approach and Objectives

Two full-scale shell impact tests, which have been reported in previous publications, e.g. [14], were conducted previously at TTC and are summarized in Table 8. The basic protocol in these tests was kept the same. A decommissioned tank car was initially standing against a rigid wall. The tank car was oriented such that the shell of the car was perpendicular to a railroad track that terminated at the wall. A ram car with an indenter protruding from its leading end was set in motion on the track and would strike the standing tank car on its shell. However, the indenter size and the impact speed were varied. Consequently, the intended objectives and outcomes of these two tests were different. In the first full-scale impact test, the commodity tank experienced plastic deformation without puncture. In the second test, the commodity tank punctured.

Table 8. Summary of Previous Full-Scale Shell Impact Tests

	Impact Speed (mph)	Indenter Dimensions			Outcome
		Width (inches)	Height (inches)	Edge Radii (inch)	
Test 1	14.0	17	23	1	Permanent deformation, no puncture
Test 2	15.1	6	6	½	Puncture

For the full-scale test with a protective panel, the objective was to demonstrate that tank integrity can be maintained at an impact speed higher than the previous tests.

3.2 Protective Panel Design, Material Selection, and Manufacturing

Based on the uniaxial compression and three-point bend testing performed in previous segments of the research program, the preferred design for the impact test was a square-tube (i.e. diamond core) sandwich panel. Because the protective panel is intended to be used against the shell of a tank car, the panel was designed to have a curved radius that conformed to the shell of the tank. However, due to the difficulty of manufacturing a curved panel with square tubes, alternative core designs, including cores with round tubes, square tubes with flattened corner faces, and X-core, were considered. Based on lower manufacturing cost and better performance, the design selected for the impact test on the tank car was a sandwich panel with a core manufactured with 3-inch round tubes.

Material selection for the panel was based on material properties and availability. A search to identify an alloy similar to 1010 steel with strength approaching Domex 100XF with higher ductility for the face sheet material was carried out. The Domex 100 XF is a low-alloy steel with yield strength of 100 ksi, tensile strength of 110 ksi, and elongation of 16 percent. The 1010 steel is a plain-carbon steel with the following minimum properties: yield strength of 44 ksi, tensile strength of 52 ksi, and elongation of 20 percent. For the core, the objective was to select the smallest thickness tube that could be easily welded. This criteria led to the selection of 3-inch O.D. tubes with a 0.083-inch thickness and a 1010 face sheet with a 0.125-inch thickness. Table 9 lists the average tensile properties measured from tensile tests conducted using three samples of each material. The numbers in parentheses represent the standard deviation for each tensile property. The tensile tests were conducted in accordance with ASTM A370 [15] and ASTM E8 [16]. The Domex sheet was included for comparison since this material was utilized in previous phases of the research program.

Table 9. Tensile Test Results for Considered Materials

	Ultimate Tensile Strength (ksi)	Yield Strength (in 2 inches) (ksi)	Elongation (in 2 inches) (%)	Reduction in Area (%)
0.118" Domex Sheet – L	119 (1.5)	106 (2.1)	17 (0.5)	68 (0.87)
0.118" Domex Sheet – T	126 (0.58)	116 (1.0)	14 (0.29)	60 (2.0)
0.083" 1010 Tube - L	67.7 (1.4)	58.2 (2.8)	22 (2.75)	70 (5.0)
0.120" 1010 Tube – L	60.7 (0.29)	48.7 (0.76)	26 (0.29)	74 (1.5)
0.120" 1010 Sheet – L	47.8 (0.38)	29.2 (0.2)	40 (1.89)	84 (2.5)
0.120" 1010 Sheet - T	47.9 (0.45)	30.3 (1.05)	40 (0.76)	87 (1.2)

NOTES: L = Longitudinal, T = Transverse

The specifications of the protective panel manufactured by CMI for the full-scale impact test are as follows:
- Panel Size: Approximately 72-inch by 72-inch
- Radius of Curvature: 55.4 inches
- Core selection: 3-inch O.D. 1010 Pipe Cores
  - Core material: Carbon Round Electric weld ASTM A513 Type 1
  - Core thickness: 0.083 inches
- Face sheet selection
  - Face sheet material: ASTM A1010 CS Type B hot rolled
  - Face sheet thickness: 0.120 inch
  - Strip face sheet inside, solid face sheet outside

The panel covered an area of the tank car shell that was approximately 6 feet (length) by 6 feet (height). This size of panel was selected for several reasons. While a larger panel would provide protection over a larger portion of the tank shell, pretest simulations indicated that larger panels had an increased likelihood of material failure occurring directly beneath the impactor. Because of this localized failure, a large panel would offer little load distribution before the impactor struck the shell of the tank. At the opposite end of the size spectrum, a panel that is only slightly larger than the impacting object would offer very little ability to blunt the impacting object owing to the small size of the panel. Additionally, more small-sized panels than large-size panels would be needed to protect the entire shell surface of the tank. The selected panel size was seen as a reasonable size for manufacturing, handling, and installation without being so large as to result in highly localized failure.

In order to fabricate a curved panel with the 55.4-inch radius, two mating fixtures were built on which to fabricate the panel. The concave fixture consisted of five concave supports with a 55.4-inch radius spaced 16 inches apart. In Figure 21, the two fixtures are shown in photos of the panel being built.

Figure 21. Manufacturing Panel for Impact Test on Concave Fixture (Left) and Convex Fixture (Right)

A series of slots for plug welding, ⅜ inches wide by 1 inch long, were laser cut on the solid face sheet and strip face sheet pieces, then the face sheets were rolled to the correct radius. The 3-inch tubes were placed on the concave fixture and tack welded together. The 3-inch wide strip face sheets, with 3-inch spacing between them, were then manually plug welded to the tubes using GMAW-P. The panel was then flipped and placed on a convex fixture so that the outer solid face sheet could be plug welded to the tubes. The plug welds were spaced 6 inches apart along the length of the tubes. The tubes were not stitch welded together because it resulted in asymmetrical deformation under loading, as shown in previous tests. The panel weighed approximately 900 pounds, with an estimated core relative density of 22.5 percent. Figure 22 shows photographs of the completed protective panel prior to it being attached to the tank car.

Figure 22. Protective Panel

3.3   Indenter Modification

As shown in Table 8, the previous full-scale tank car impact testing used a 6-inch by 6-inch indenter. CMI built a cap that was placed over the existing 6-inch by 6-inch indenter in order to adjust its impact footprint. Figure 23 shows schematics of the retrofit cap. The cap face was made with A514 steel. The sides of the cap and the gussets were made with A36 steel. The weld filler was ER110S-1. This modification resulted in a 12-inch by 12-inch indenter with a 1-inch radius. Figure 24 shows photographs of the retrofitted indenter. There are no welds between the 12-inch by 12-inch cap and the 6-inch by 6-inch indenter. That is, contact is the only load transfer mechanism. The cap was designed to be removed to permit the 6-inch by 6-inch indenter to be utilized for any potential future testing programs.

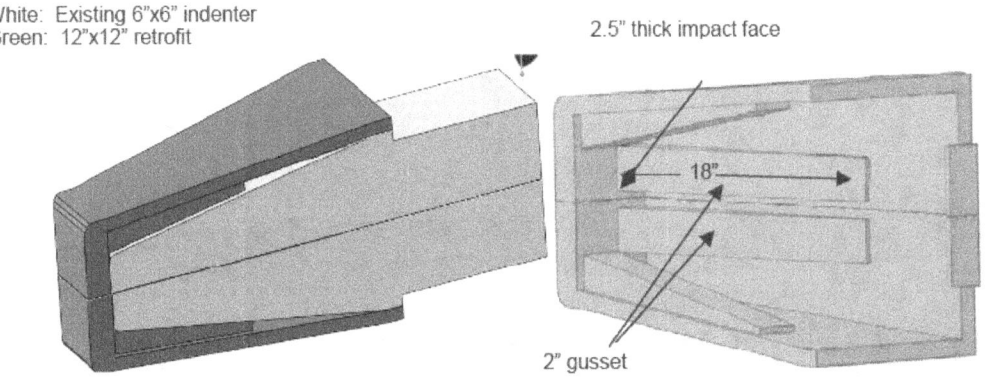

Figure 23. Modification of 6-Inch by 6-Inch Indenter

Figure 24. Photos of Indenter Cap on 6-Inch by 6-Inch Indenter

3.4 Test Setup

The tank car used in the full-scale testing was a decommissioned DOT105J500W that was previously used in service to carry liquid chlorine. Figure 25 shows a photograph of the test setup used in the impact test. The tank car with the protective panel was positioned with one side against a 3-inch steel plate attached to a concrete retaining wall, perpendicular to the track that the ram car (shown at right) would travel on. The commodity-carrying tank was insulated with approximately 4 inches of fiberglass and ceramic fiber insulation. The fiberglass and insulation were covered by a thin steel outer jacket. The jacket and thermal protection were kept intact for the test, with the panel installed outside of the jacket. The tank car was filled 90 percent with water and then pressurized to 100 psi.

Figure 25. Test Setup – View from East (Left) Side

The wheels of the tank car were removed and replaced with heavy rectangular tube assemblies. This test car was then placed on two skids, shown in Figure 26. Four short I-beam sections connected the tank body bolster and skids (Figure 27). The tank car with the skids was placed on 1-inch steel plates laid on the ground. The resulting skid system was designed to minimize the test car rollback and to allow the tank car and skids to slide on the steel plates during the impact.

32

Figure 26. Skid System

Figure 27. Welded Beam Connecting the Tank Car to the Skid System

The protective panel was hung in the front and outside of the tank car outer jacket from the manhole using a cable that ran through the sixth tube. An additional cable with slack was used on the seventh tube to prevent the panel from falling to the ground in the event that the first cable broke. The panel hung freely against the tank car outer jacket to allow the panel to deflect freely during the impact. The panel hanging against the tank is shown in Figure 28.

Figure 28. Test Setup – View from West (Right) Side

Welding the panel to the jacket was considered as an attachment option, but it was believed that this would result in an overly-stiff support condition. If the panel was not able to flex in response to the impact, the panel would likely experience highly-localized puncture around the perimeter of the impactor head. This localized failure would prevent the panel from distributing the impact load over an area of the tank shell larger than the impactor. The selected mounting attachment scheme was intentionally chosen to permit the panel to flex and deform in response to the striking impactor. Because of the irregularity of the outer jacket, the panel did not rest uniformly against the tank car. There was an approximately 1-inch gap between the panel and the car at both of its ends along the radius. The panel and car rested with no gaps at their centerlines and almost 2 feet above and below that area.

3.5 Instrumentation

Eleven accelerometers and two speed sensors were installed on the ram car. Two pressure transducers measured tank pressure at the pressure relief valves on the tank car. Three high-speed (HS) cameras and four high-definition (HD) video cameras documented the impact. Table 10 summarizes the types of instrumentation and the channel counts.

Table 10. Instrumentation Summary

Type of Instrumentation	Channel Count
Accelerometers	11
Speed Sensors	2
Pressure Transducers	2
Total Data Channels	**15**
Digital Video	7 Cameras (3 HS and 4 HD)

3.5.1 Ram Car Accelerometers and Speed Sensors

Triaxial accelerometers were placed at the two ends and at the center along the ram car centerline. Two longitudinal accelerometers were placed on the left and right sides of the middle of the ram car. There were a total of 11 accelerometers installed on the ram car. The typical scale factor calibration error for the accelerometers used was 2 percent. There were two speed sensors installed on the ram car, one on the left and one on the right. Figure 29 illustrates the sensor locations. Table 11 shows the details of the accelerometers installed on the ram car.

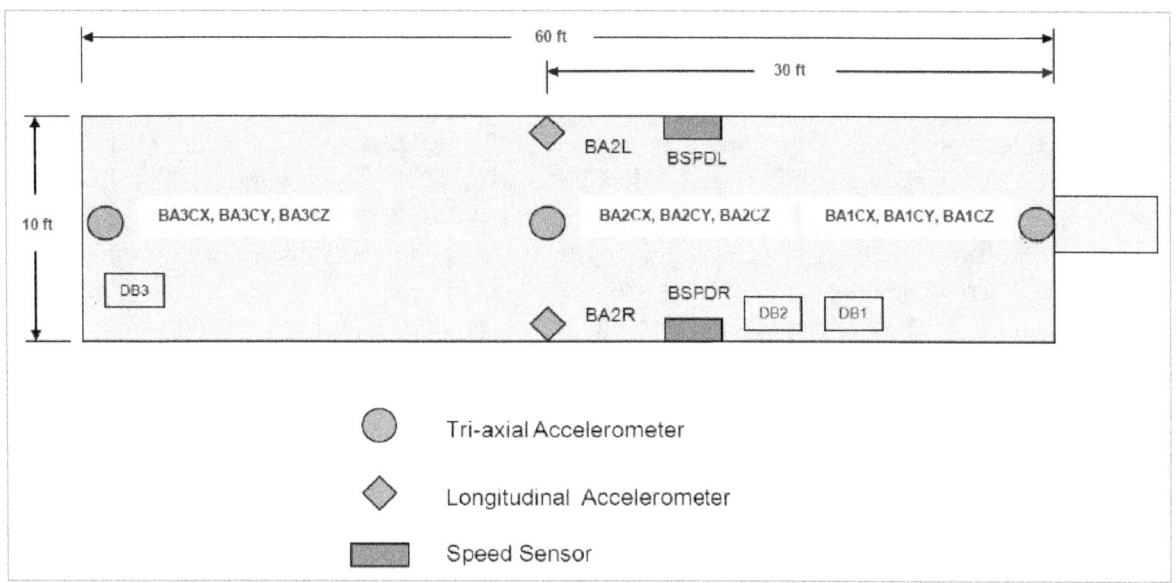

Figure 29. Accelerometer Locations on Ram Car

Table 11. Ram Car Accelerometers

Channel Name	Sensor Description	Range
BA1CX	Leading end, Centerline, X Accelerometer	100g
BA1CY	Leading end, Centerline, Y Accelerometer	100g
BA1CZ	Leading, Centerline, Z Accelerometer	100g
BA2LX	Middle, Left Side X Accelerometer	100g
BA2CX	Middle, Centerline, X Accelerometer	50g
BA2CY	Middle, Centerline, Y Accelerometer	50g
BA2CZ	Middle, Centerline, Z Accelerometer	50g
BA2RX	Middle, Right Side X Accelerometer	100g
BA3CX	Trailing end, Centerline, X Accelerometer	200g
BA3CY	Trailing end, Centerline, Y Accelerometer	100g
BA3CZ	Trailing end, Centerline, Z Accelerometer	200g

35

3.5.2 Tank Car Pressure Transducers

Two pressure transducers were attached to the pressure relief valves on the manway to measure the internal pressure in the tank during the impact. Table 12 lists the pressure transducers.

Table 12. Pressure Transducers

Channel Name	Sensor Description	Range (psi)
TRP1	Low-range pressure transducer	600
TRP2	High-range pressure transducer	1,200

3.5.3 Speed Sensors

Redundant speed sensors measured the impact speed of the ram car when it was within 12 inches of the impact point. The speed traps used reflector-based sensors. The ground-based reflectors were separated by a known distance, and vehicle-based light sensors were triggered as the ram car passed over the reflectors. The last reflector was within 10 inches of the impact point. The time interval between passing the reflectors was recorded. Speed was then calculated from distance and time. The backup speed measurement was recorded with a handheld radar gun.

3.5.4 Real-Time Photography and Targets

Three HS and four real-time HD video cameras documented the impact event. Figure 30 and Figure 31 show schematics of the camera position setup. All HS cameras are crashworthy and rated for peak accelerations of 100 g.

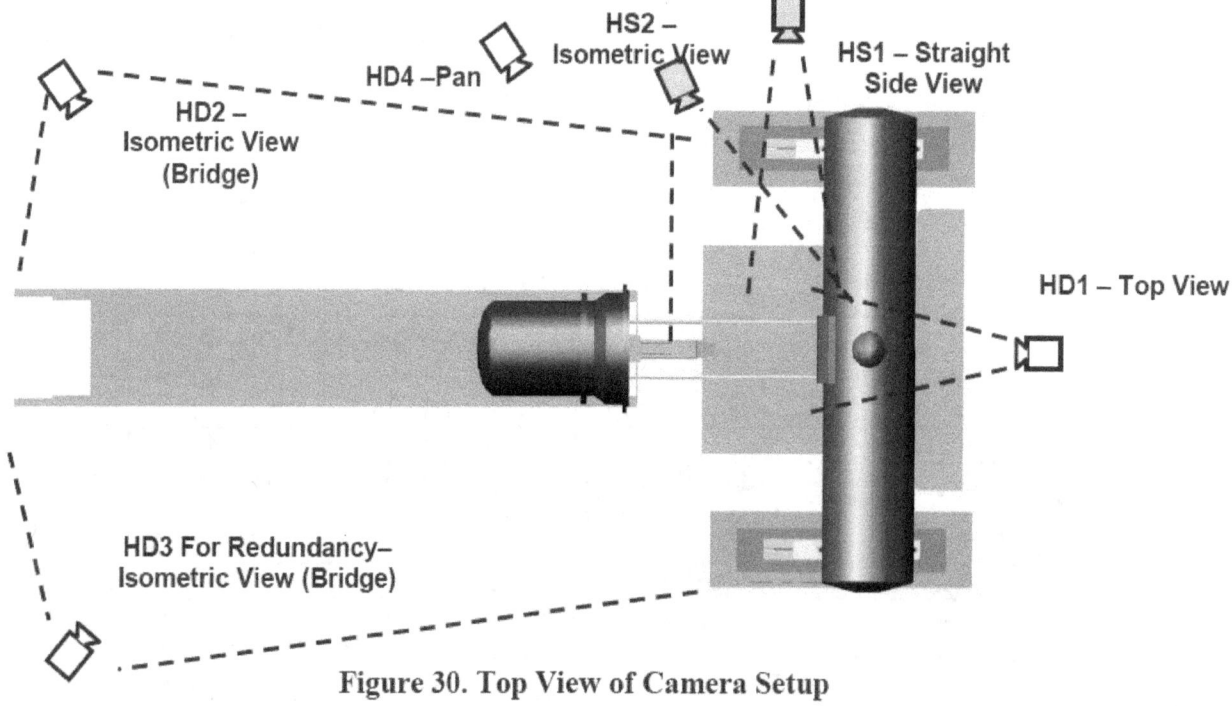

Figure 30. Top View of Camera Setup

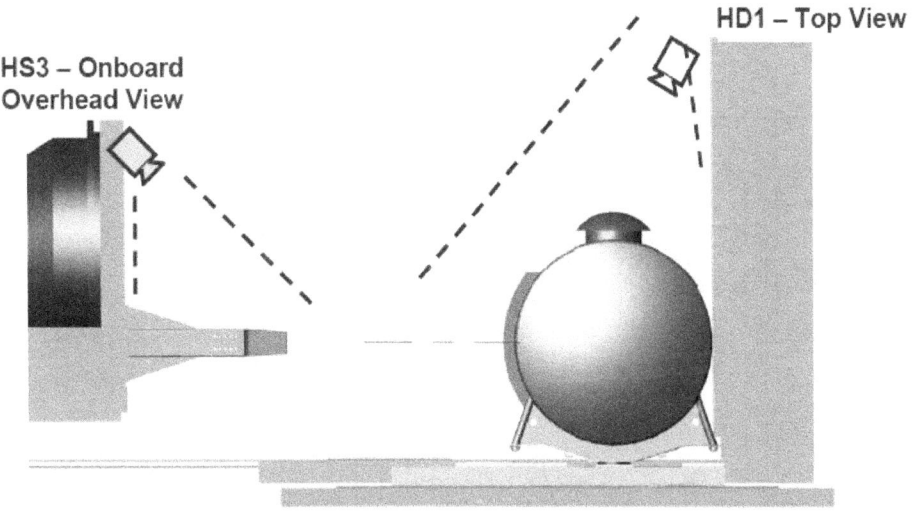

Figure 31. Side View of Camera Setup

The ram car, the protective panel, and the impact barrier were painted light gray. The tip of the indenter was painted red. High-contrast targets were applied to the ram car, the indenter, the protective panel, and at select ground reference points to aid in video analysis, should video analysis be necessary. Figure 32 through Figure 35 show the target locations on the ram car and on the tank car with the protective panel.

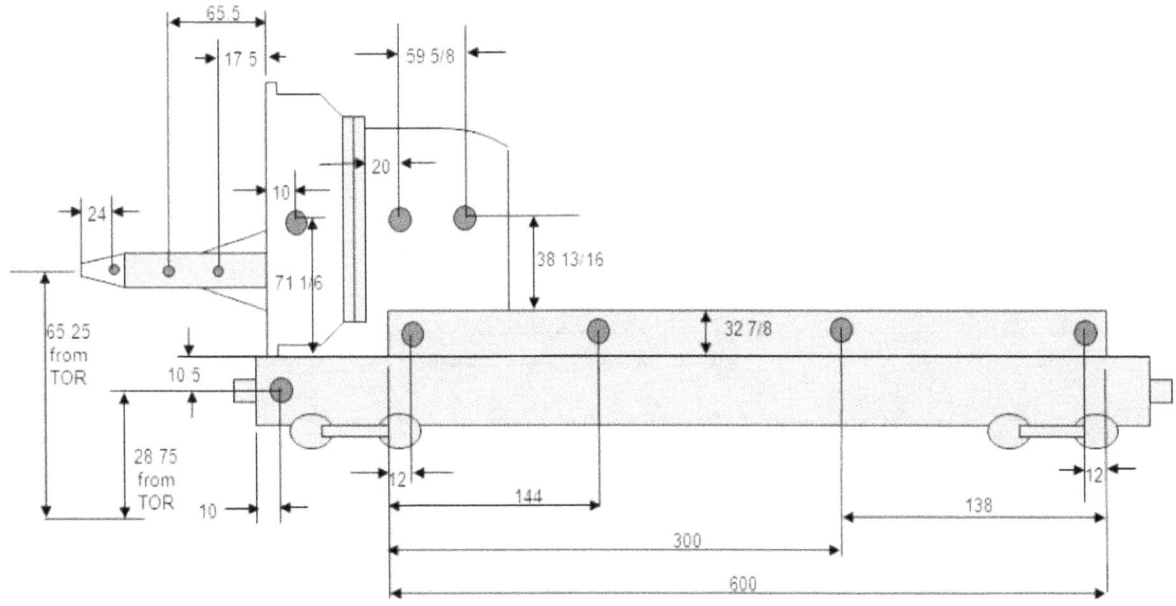

Figure 32. Side View of Target Locations on Ram Car

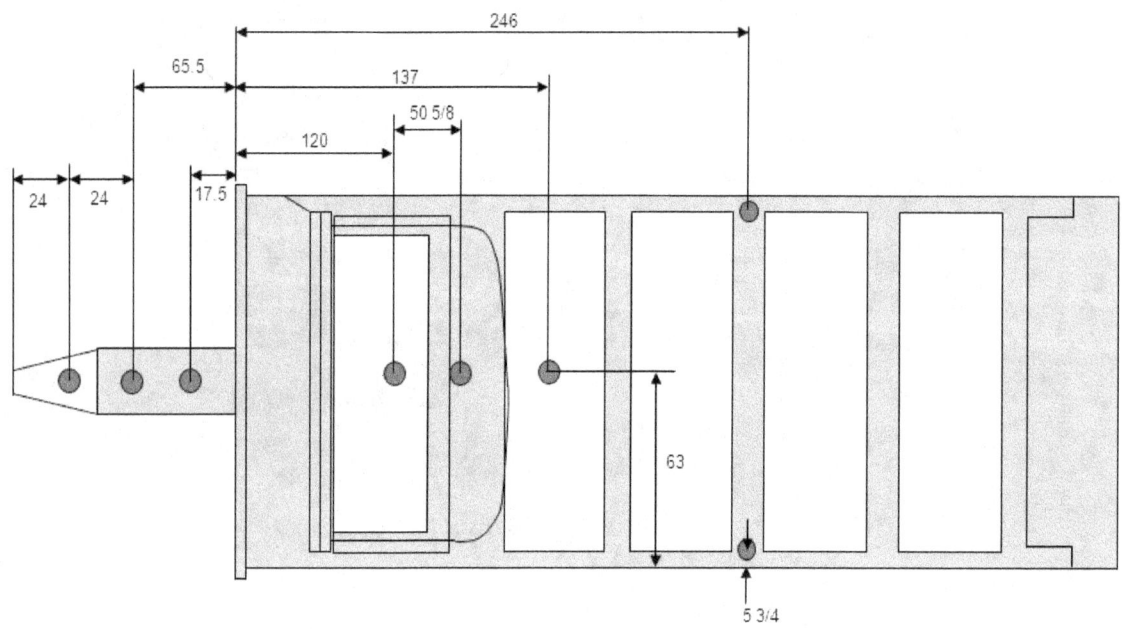

Figure 33. Top View of Target Locations on Ram Car

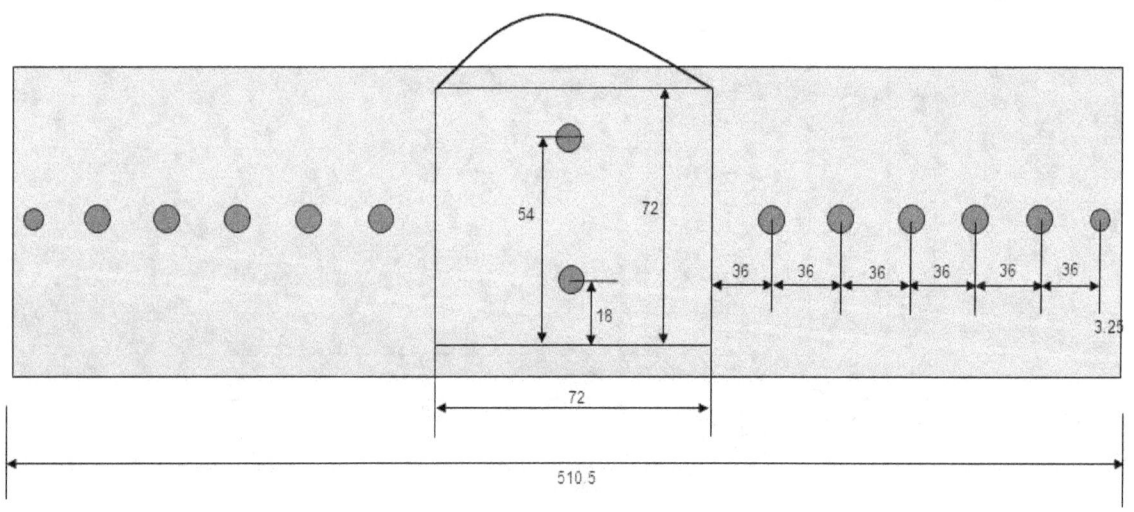

Figure 34. Side View of Target Locations on Tank Car and Protective Panel

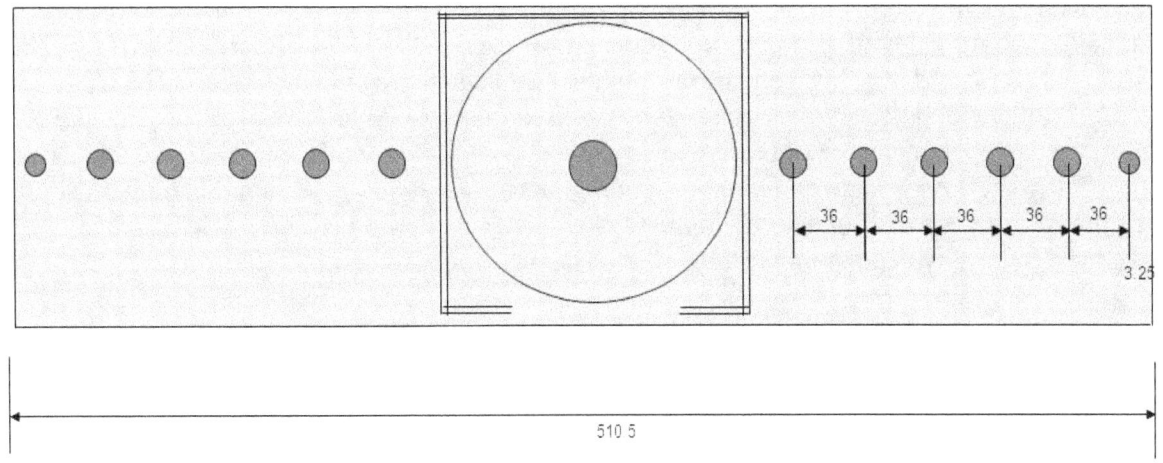

Figure 35. Top View of Target Locations on Tank Car

3.5.5 Special Considerations for Protecting Equipment

Shielding was provided for all external instrumentation near the point of impact. The intent was to provide protection from high-velocity liquid in case the tank ruptured. For sensors such as accelerometers, welded or bolted shields were used. For cameras near the impact zone, high-strength clear plastic shells, like the one shown in Figure 36, were used.

Figure 36. Protective Shell for Onboard HS Camera

3.5.6 Data Acquisition

A set of 8-channel battery-powered onboard data acquisition systems recorded data from instrumentation mounted on the ram car. These systems provided excitation to the instrumentation, analog antialiasing filtering of the signals, analog-to-digital conversion, and recording of each data stream. A similar set of ground-based data acquisition systems recorded data from the pressure transducers on the tank car.

The data acquisition systems were GMH Engineering DataBRICK Model II units [17]. Data acquisition complied with the appropriate sections of SAE J211/1 [18]. Data from each channel was antialias filtered at 1,735 hertz (Hz) and then sampled and recorded at 12,800 Hz. Data recorded on the DataBRICK units were synchronized to time zero at initial impact. The time reference came from closure of tape switches installed on the front of the test vehicle. Each DataBRICK unit is ruggedized for shock loading up to at least 100 g. Onboard battery power was provided by GMH Engineering in the form of 1.7 A-hr 14.4 Volt NiCad Packs. Tape Switches, Inc., provided the model 1201-131-A tape switches for event initial contact.

Software in the DataBRICK units was used to preset zero levels for all acceleration channels. The DataBRICK units were set to record 1 second of data before the initial impact and 4 seconds of data after the initial impact.

3.6   Test Results and Observations

The test car was impacted by a 12-inch by 12-inch square indenter attached to a moving ram car with a total weight of 295,725 pounds. The ram car was released by a locomotive from rest at 1,600 feet away from the impact barrier. The track was inclined so that the ram car picked up speed as it traveled toward the standing tank car. The speed of the ram car when it struck the test car was 17.8 mph. The impact location was the center of the side of the tank car and the panel. Figure 37 shows a series of still images taken from video of the impact test. This image shows the progress of the ram car as it strikes the panel-equipped car, causes deformation of the car, and is eventually propelled backward following rebound of the tank car.

| Preimpact | During Impact | Postimpact |

Figure 37. Series of Images Showing Side Impact Progression

The ram caused significant deformation to both the protective panel and the tank shell. The tank was both deformed and displaced by the impact. The tank did not puncture during this test, but successfully withstood the impact with its lading intact. The ram car was eventually propelled backward (i.e. opposite its initial direction of travel) as the tank car recovered elastically following the collision. Figure 38 shows a photograph of the tank car with the protective panel after impact. The spacing between targets on the side of the shell is indicated on this figure.

Figure 38. Tank Car and Panel after Impact

The ram car had air brakes that were designed to activate 2 seconds after the ram impacted the tank car to assure that the ram car did not rebound off the tank car, move up the incline, and then roll back into the tank car a second time. The test car bounced back 112 feet before the automatic brakes were tripped.

The test parameters for the 105J500W tank car were:
- Tank car number   DCLX3050
- Tank car LT WT (empty)   81,700 pounds
- Outage   10%
- Tank capacity   17,445 gal
- Fill fluid   water
- Internal pressure   100 psi
- Tank car height (center to top of rail)   64.5 in.

The test parameters for the ram car were:
- Ram car weight   295,725 pounds
- Ram car initial speed   17.8 mph
- Indenter height (center to top of rail)   65.25 in.
- Ram car energy (derived)   3.13 million foot-pounds

The ambient conditions at the time of test were:
- Wind speed   5 mph NNE
- Ambient temperature   50°F
- Humidity   74%
- Barometric pressure   29.53 inches Hg

When the panel was impacted, the center of the panel crushed inward and the left and right edges of the panel buckled and pulled away from the tank car. The front face sheet stretched in an area from the left to right edge of the panel and approximately 1 foot above and below the impact. In some of the area that stretched and buckled, the plug welds on the top face sheet failed, and the front face sheet tore at the edges of the indenter, as seen in Figure 39.

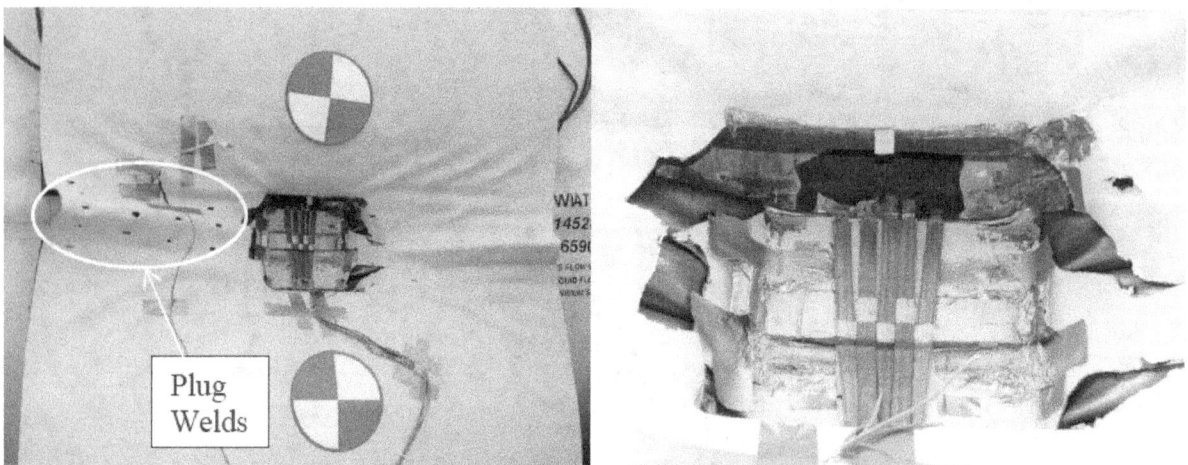

Figure 39. Damage on Protective Panel – Impact Side

The round pipes crushed in the area beneath the indenter—so much so that the walls of the pipes were touching and one severed near the edge of the impact. The outer core, on the left and right edges of the panel, deformed but the deformation was not as severe as it was in the center of the panel. On the edges, the pipes became oblong and some had a flattened edge adjacent to the tank car. Figure 40 shows the deformation of the panel from the side views.

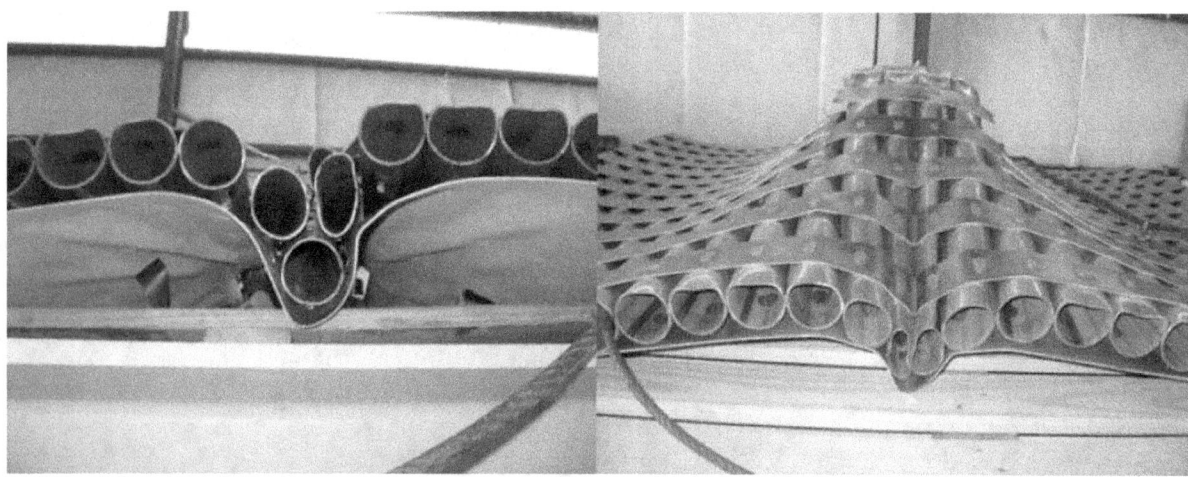

Figure 40. Damage on Protective Panel – Left and Right Sides

The back of the panel was bowed, which is shown in Figure 41. Some of the strips that made up the back face sheet tore at the edges of the indenter. The back of the pipes beneath the indenter were flattened.

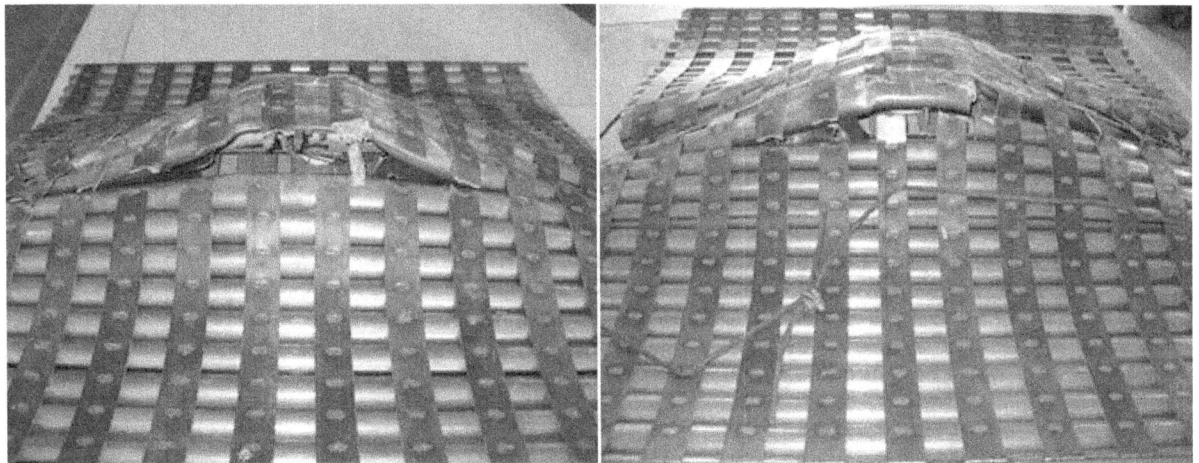

Figure 41. Damage on Back of Protective Panel

Damage to the steel jacket was exposed after removing the protective panel from the side of the tank (Figure 42). This figure also shows the spacing between targets on the side of the tank shell.

Figure 42. Dent in the Jacket

After removing the steel jacket and the insulation, damage to the commodity-carrying tank was observed in the form of permanent dent without puncture (Figure 43). Moreover, there were no visible signs that water had leaked. The permanent dent in the commodity-carrying tank was approximately 11.5 inches deep and at least 160 inches long.

Figure 43. Deformation of Commodity Tank

The center of the indenter impacted the panel directly over a weld seam on the tank car—this represents a worst case scenario. In the bottom section of the tank car, along the weld, there was some indication that the weld was beginning to fail in the HAZ area. Furthermore, a surface crack was found in the weld seam (Figure 44).

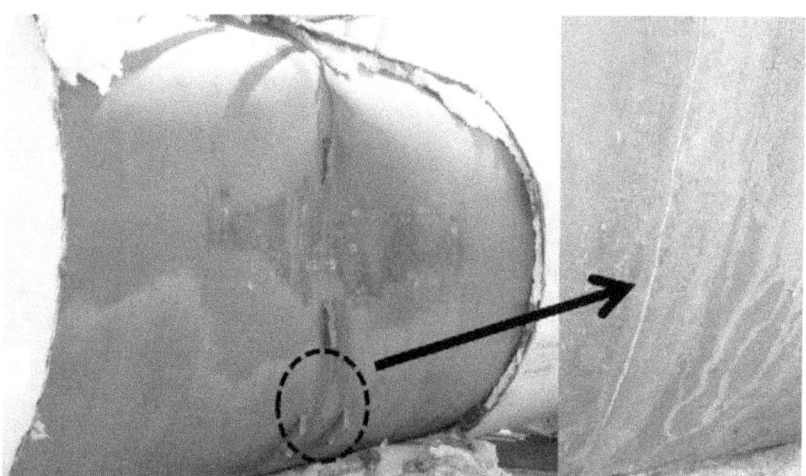

Figure 44. Surface Crack on the Tank Car

During the impact, the tank car was pressed between the ram car and the retaining wall. Once the ram car's forward motion had stopped, the tank car began to recover some of its elastic energy. This caused both the tank car and the ram car to rebound away from the retaining wall. The tank car rebounded during the impact and left more than 12 inches between the tank car and the impact barrier following the test (Figure 45).

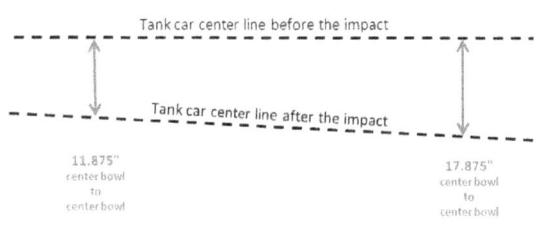

Figure 45. Tank Car Placement after Impact

Instrumentation on the ram car provided data for calculation of the ram force and ram car energy. Signals from three ram car longitudinal accelerometers, BA2CX, BA2LX, and BA2RX were averaged to obtain the ram car acceleration (Figure 46). These acceleration signals were filtered with a Butterworth 4-pole phaseless low-pass filter that had a corner frequency of 100 Hz. Maximum deceleration was approximately 6.0 g, as shown in Figure 46. In the figure, a time of 0 seconds corresponds to the initial contact between ram face and protective panel.

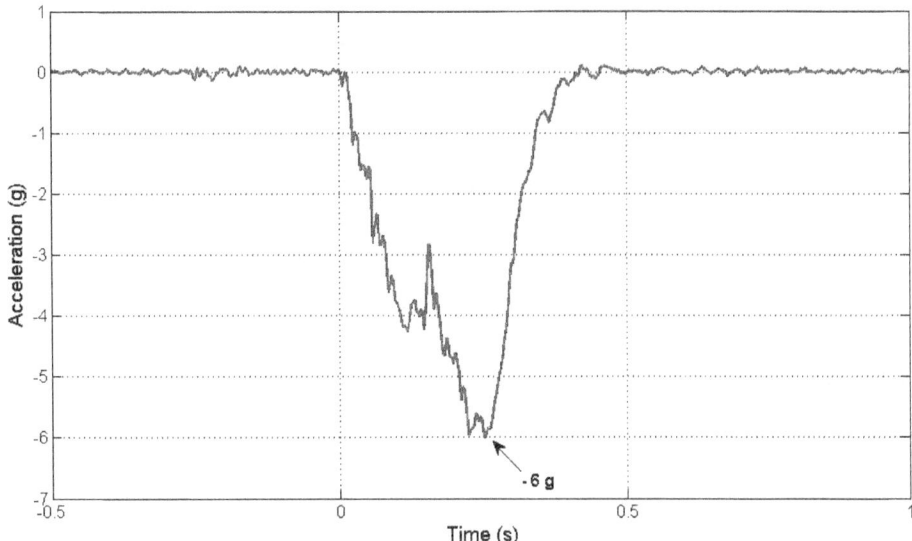

Figure 46. Ram Car Acceleration

Longitudinal force on the ram car was calculated as the product of ram car mass and acceleration. Figure 47 shows ram car force as a function of time. The longitudinal force on the ram car was produced by the moving ram contact with the tank car. The maximum force was approximately 1.8 million pounds.

45

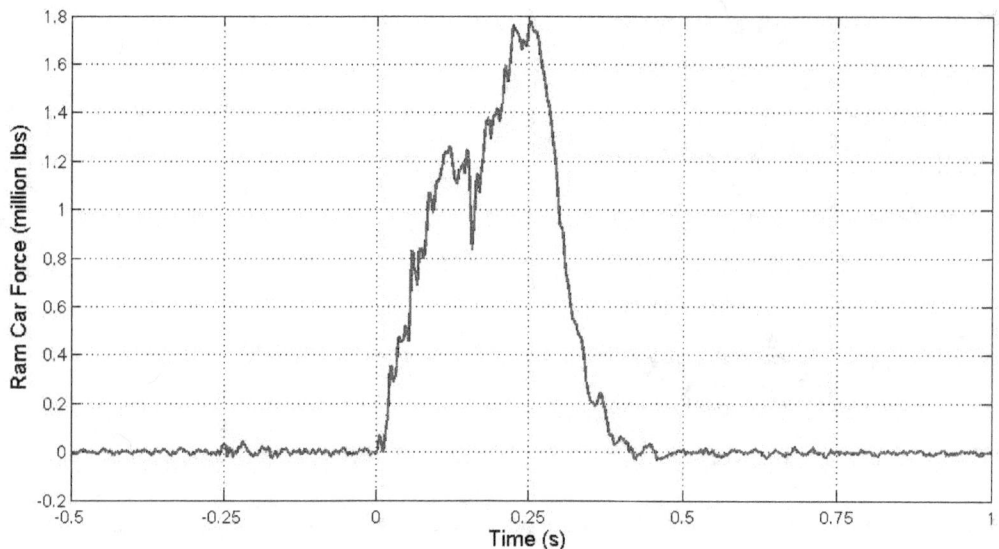

Figure 47. Ram Car Force

The ram car's velocity was computed by integrating and averaging the three acceleration signals identified above. The initial speed of the ram car (just prior to impact) was measured independent of the accelerometers. Figure 48 shows the velocity versus time behavior for the ram car. The ram car had an initial speed of 17.8 mph and a rebound speed of 9.3 mph. The calculated initial and rebound speed agreed with the data from the speed sensors and the speed gun.

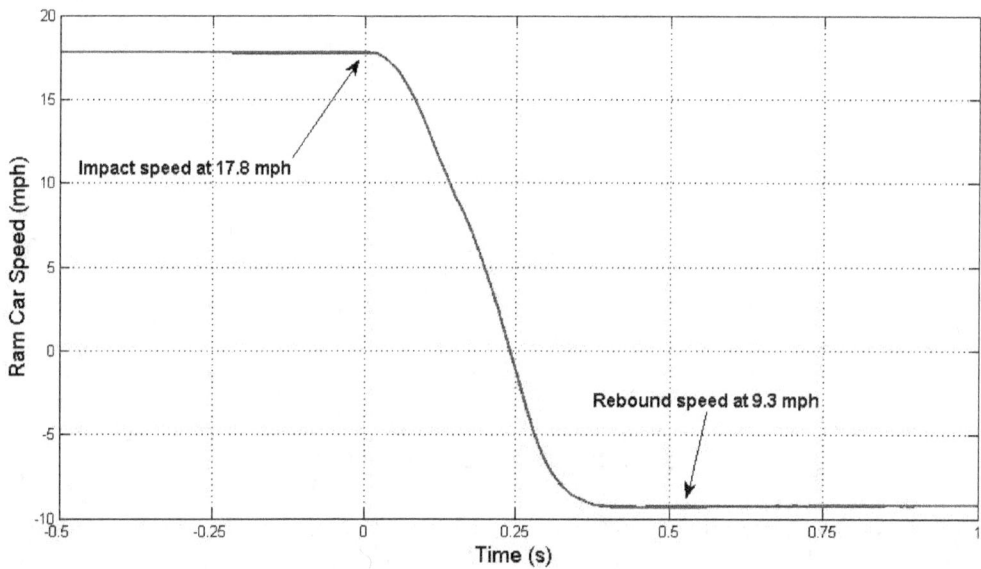

Figure 48. Ram Car Speed during Impact

Ram car longitudinal travel was computed by twice integrating the three acceleration signals. Figure 49 is a plot of the ram car longitudinal travel versus time. The ram made initial contact with the protective panel at a time of 0 seconds. This corresponds to a ram car longitudinal travel distance of 0 inches. This figure shows the maximum indentation of 47.41 inches, which agreed with the analysis of the side-view HS video. Following removal of the jacket and insulation, the permanent indentation in the tank was found to be approximately 11.5 inches deep.

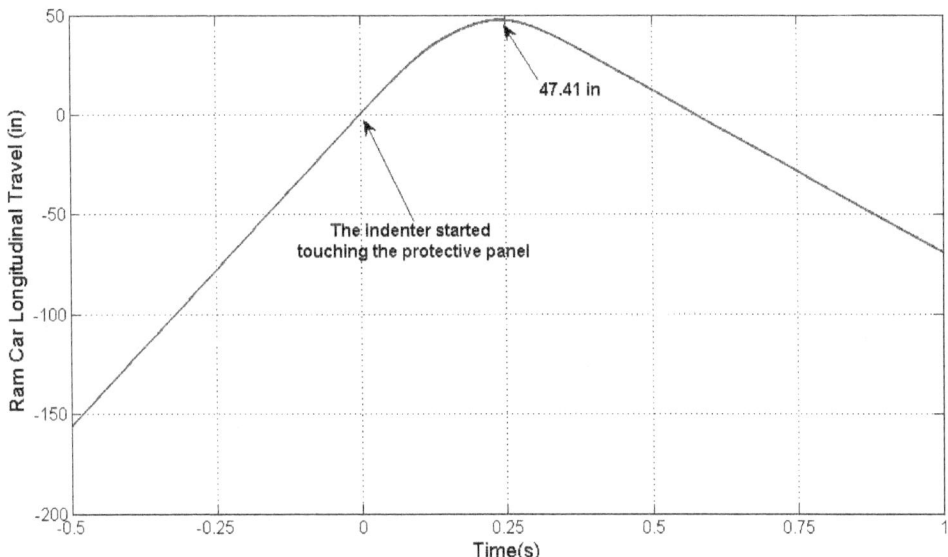

Figure 49. Ram Car Longitudinal Travel

Ram car kinetic energy was computed from the following equation:

$$E = \frac{1}{2} m v^2$$

Based upon the mass of the ram car and an impact speed of 17.8 mph, the kinetic energy of the ram car at the time of impact was calculated as 3.13 million foot-pounds. Figure 50 shows a plot of kinetic energy versus time for the ram car from a time prior to impact through rebound of the ram car. The kinetic energy of the ram car decreases as the ram is slowed during the impact, reaching a minimum value of 0 foot-pounds at the time of maximum indentation. As the ram car begins to accelerate backward by elastic recovery of the tank car, the kinetic energy begins to climb. As the ram car is propelled backward from the tank car it has a kinetic energy of approximately 0.85 million foot-pounds. The difference between initial and final kinetic energy of the ram car is approximately 2.28 million foot-pounds. This energy corresponds to the energy that was dissipated by the tank car and protective panel.

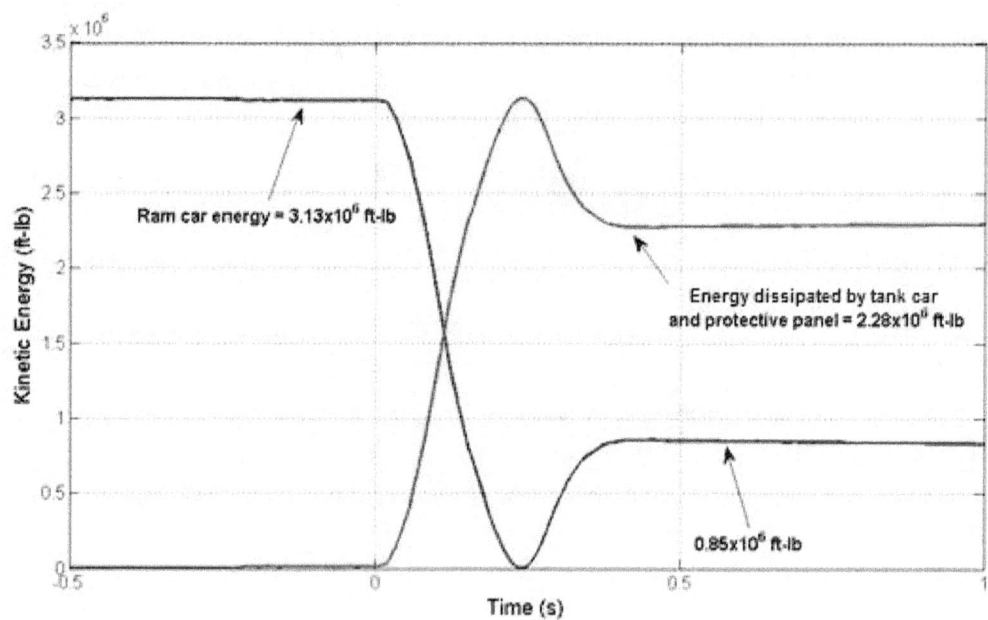

Figure 50. Kinetic Energy versus Time

Figure 51 shows the ram car force versus travel distance. The maximum force imparted to the ram car occurs at the period of maximum forward travel. As the ram car is forced backward, the force decreases until the ram has separated from the tank car and is moving backward along the track.

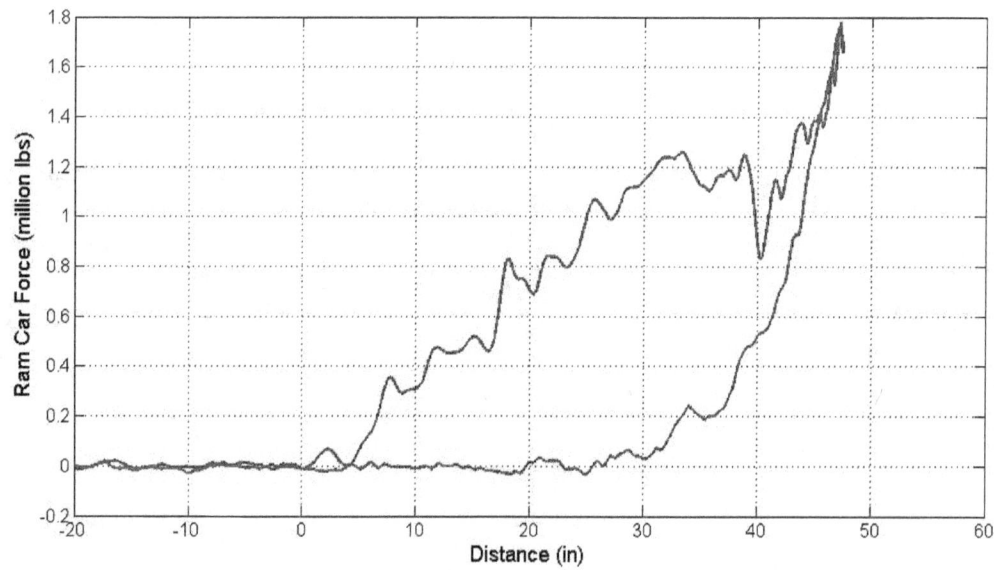

Figure 51. Ram Car Force versus Distance

48

4. Summary

This report describes research conducted over a three-year span in which sandwich structure technology was investigated as a means to provide protection to railroad tank cars against the threat of an object impacting the side of the tank. This research may be divided into two phases. The first phase was basic research with the objectives to: (1) examine fabrication and manufacturing issues associated with sandwich structures, (2) observe the deformation behavior of flat, welded steel sandwich panels under quasi-static loading, (3) confirm analytical and computational modeling efforts, and (4) rank and select candidate core geometries for dynamic impact testing. Fabrication and manufacturing issues were material selection for the sandwich panel components (face sheets and core geometries) as well as welding processes to build the panels. Focus was given to off-the-shelf materials because of their availability in the desired quantities. Flat, welded steel sandwich panels with candidate cores and materials were subjected to two types of quasi-static loading conditions: (1) uniaxial compression, and (2) bending with an indenter. Observations and results from these tests were described in a previous report [4]. This report also included computational analyses to complement the testing effort.

The second phase of research was the design of a curved, welded steel sandwich panel to protect an actual railroad tank car during a full-scale impact test. Based on the observations and results of the basic research phase, a curved sandwich panel was built with 3-inch OD pipe cores, a solid outer face sheet, and strips for the inner face sheet. As shown in Figure 52, the panel measured approximately 6 feet by 6 feet. The core material was ASTM A513 steel with a thickness of 0.086 inches. The face sheet material was ASTM A1010 with a thickness of 0.120 inch. The cores were attached to the face sheets by gas metal arc welding (GMAW). The protective panel weighed approximately 900 pounds.

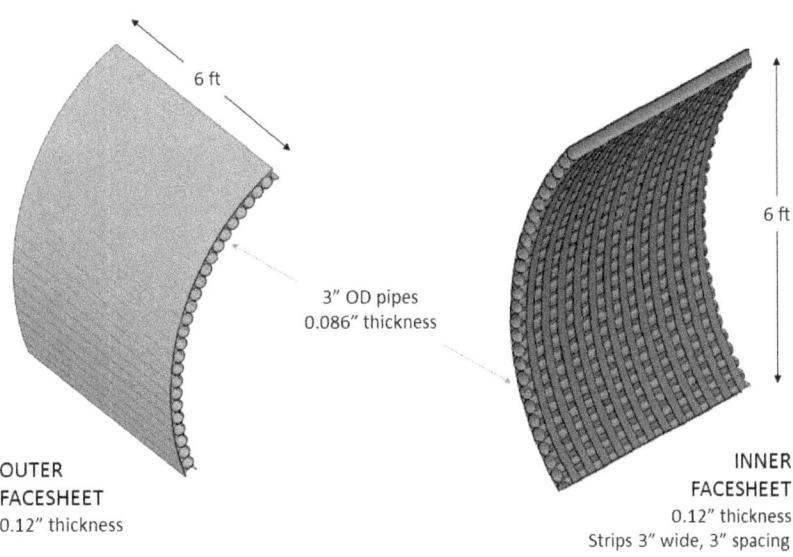

Figure 52. Schematic of Protective Panel used in Full-scale Impact Test

The protective panel was hung in front and outside of a decommissioned tank car, which was braced against a concrete barrier. The tank car and panel were struck by a 12" x 12" indenter mounted to a ram car moving with an initial kinetic energy of approximately 3.13 million foot-pounds. The impact resulted in permanent deformation to both the protective panel and the tank car. However, the tank car did not puncture and all lading (water) was contained throughout the impact. The ram car was propelled backward following the impact at a speed of approximately 9.3 mph.

5. Discussion

In a collision event, momentum or kinetic energy is transferred from the moving object to other initially stationary objects in the overall system. In the full-scale shell impact test described in this report, the exchange of momentum or kinetic energy occurs among the various system components that include the protective panel, the outer jacket, the commodity-carrying tank, and the lading inside the tank.

The sandwich construction of the protective panel is designed to dissipate the kinetic energy and to distribute the impact load over a larger footprint than that of the indenter. Moreover, the compliance or flexibility of the sandwich panel allows for appreciable energy loss, in terms of dissipation and absorption. The energy loss is manifested through damage in the form of creating fracture surfaces or permanent deformation. In the full-scale test, for example, fractures of the welds and breaking of the strip face sheets were observed in the protective panel after impact. In addition, permanent deformation of the outer jacket and the commodity tank were also observed.

In the full-scale impact test described in Section 3, the ram car weight was 295,725 pounds and the impact speed was 17.8 mph. The corresponding kinetic energy is more than 3 million foot-pounds. In an attempt to envision the magnitude of this level of energy, Figure 53 shows other collision scenarios that generate the same level of kinetic energy. That is, a passenger car (assumed to weigh 160,000 pounds) traveling at 24.2 mph produces the same kinetic energy as the ram car impacting the tank car with the protective panel in the full-scale test. Similarly, an empty tank car (assumed to weigh 81,700 pounds) moving at a speed of 33.9 mph also translates to the same level of kinetic energy.

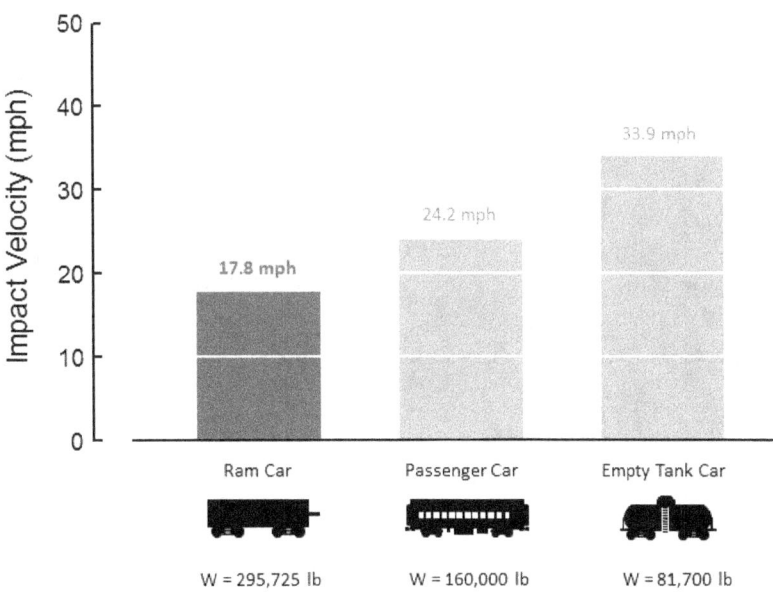

Figure 53. Impact Scenarios with Equivalent Kinetic Energy

Table 13 indicates that the impact speed achieved in the most recent test (i.e. 17.8 mph) is the highest impact speed of the three full-scale tank car impact tests conducted at TTC. The table also indicates that the indenter dimensions in each of the tests were different. Therefore, in addition to ram car weight and impact speed, another key factor that affects the likelihood of whether the commodity-carrying tank will puncture in the event of an impact is the size of the indenter. Damage from relatively small indenters is highly localized, and is concentrated near the corners of the indenter face. For relatively larger indenters, the overall tank "system" is engaged to help dissipate the kinetic energy from impact. Finite element simulations of full-scale tank car shell impacts such as those conducted at TTC suggest that the distinction between relatively small and large indenters is in the range between the 6-inch by 6-inch and the 12-inch by 12-inch indenters.

Table 13. Summary of Full-scale Tank Car Shell Impact Tests Conducted at TTC

| | Impact Speed (mph) | Indenter Dimensions | | | Outcome |
		Width (inches)	Height (inches)	Edge Radii (inch)	
Test 1	14.0	17	23	1	Permanent deformation, no puncture
Test 2	15.1	6	6	½	Puncture
Test 3*	17.8	12	12	1	Permanent deformation, no puncture

* With protective panel

Referring to Figure 52, the protective panel used in the most recent full-scale test covered an area of the tank car shell approximately six feet in length by six feet in height. The size of the panel was selected for several reasons. While a larger panel would provide protection over a larger portion of the tank shell, pretest finite element simulations suggested that larger panels had an increased likelihood of material failure occurring directly beneath the indenter. Because of this localized failure, a large panel would offer little load distribution before the indenter strikes the shell of the tank. At the opposite end of the size spectrum, a panel that is only slightly larger than the impacting object would offer very little ability to blunt the impacting object owing to the small size of the panel. Additionally, if the protection scheme were envisioned to cover the entire shell surface of the tank, a smaller panel would require more instances to be installed. The selected panel size was seen as a reasonable size for manufacturing, handling, and installation without being so large as to result in highly localized failure.

Using a 6-foot by 6-foot curved panel to protect the side of a tank car resembles using a half-height shield to protect the end or the head of a tank car. Given the dramatically improved safety performance of tank cars after head protection requirements were instituted, this resemblance leads to the notion of using protective panels based on sandwich structure technology to retrofit existing tank cars against the threat of side of shell impacts. A possible strategy to optimize the costs, risks, and benefits associated with shell protection might be partial protection of the tank. For example, some benefit, balanced against cost and risk, could be realized from protecting only the bottom half of the tank since accident statistics indicate that shell punctures are more likely to occur along the lower half of the tank. Partial protection schemes are outlined in Appendix A.

One area that remains open in terms of applying sandwich structure technology to protect railroad tank cars against shell puncture is how to effectively attach the protective panel to the tank structure. The attachments would need to be compliant or flexible in order to mitigate localized failures. Various concepts are outlined in Appendix B of this report, but ultimately the expertise and the experience of tank car manufacturers will be required to develop an appropriate design.

Absorbing and dissipating 3 million foot-pounds of energy represents a formidable challenge because the design of such a system is constrained by the maximum allowable weight and clearance standards for rail cars. The effect of weight and space budgets on designs to improve the safety performance of tank cars has been discussed in previous work [6]. The protective panel designed and built for the full-scale impact test weighed approximately 900 pounds. If such panels covered the entire tank car shell, the resulting shell protection system would be within weight and space limitations for tank cars built to 286,000-pound gross weights. The observations and results from the research described in this report suggest that sandwich structure technology can, in principle, be applied to provide protection to the tank car shell in the event of a shell impact. Moreover, protection against puncture is essential for tank cars carrying those materials with the greatest potential to harm humans and the environment if released.

6.   References

1. Bureau of Explosives (BOE), *Annual Report of Hazardous Materials Transported by Rail: Calendar Year 2011.* Association of American Railroads, Washington, D.C. (2012).
2. Tyrell, D., Jeong, D., Jacobsen, K., Martinez, E., "Improved Tank Car Safety Research," *Proceedings of the 2007 ASME Rail Transportation Division Fall Technical Conference, RTDF2007-46013*, Chicago, IL, September 2007.
3. Treichel, T., "List of Accident-Caused Releases of Toxic Inhalation Hazard (TIH) Materials from Tank Cars, 1965-2005," RSI-AAR Railroad Tank Car Safety Research and Test Project, Report No, RA 06-05 (2006)
4. Jeong, D.Y., Carolan, M.E., Perlman, A.B., Tang, Y.H., "Deformation Behavior of Welded Steel Sandwich Panels Under Quasi-Static Loading," Volpe National Transportation Systems Center Final Report, DOT/FRA/ORD-11/06, March 2011.
5. Carolan, M.E., Jeong, D.Y., Perlman, A.B., Tang, Y.H., "Deformation Behavior of Welded Steel Sandwich Panels Under Quasi-Static Loading," *Proceedings of the ASME/ASCE/IEEE 2011 Joint Rail Conference, JRC2011-56054*, Pueblo, CO, March 2011.
6. Tyrell, D., Jacobsen, K., Talamini, B., Carolan, M., "Developing Strategies for Maintaining Tank Car Integrity During Train Accidents," *Proceedings of the 2007 ASME Rail Transportation Division Fall Technical Conference, RTDF2007-46015*, Chicago, IL, September 2007.
7. http://www.efunda.com/materials/alloys/alloy_home/show_alloy_found.cfm?ID=AISI_4130&show_prop=all&Page_Title=AISI%204130
8. http://www.efunda.com/materials/alloys/carbon_steels/show_carbon.cfm?ID=AISI_1010&prop=all&Page_Title=AISI%201010
9. Jones, J., Quote from Weldedtube (2008)
10. http://www.leecosteel.com/products/high-strength-low-alloy-structural/hsla-structural-quality/a656-hsla-steel.html
11. http://www.ssab.com/Global/Domex/Datasheets/en/444_Domex%20100%20XF.pdf
12. Association of American Railroads, AAR Manual of Standards and Recommended Practices and Specifications for Tank Cars, M-1002, Appendix M.
13. Abernathy, M., Quote from Bull Moose Tube (2008)
14. Tang, Y.H., Yu, H., Gordon, J.E., Priante, M., Jeong, D.Y., Tyrell, D.C., Perlman, A.B., "Analyses of full-scale tank car shell impact tests," *Proceedings of the 2007 ASME Rail Transportation Division Fall Technical Conference, RTDF2007-46010*, Chicago, IL, September 2007.
15. ASTM Standard A370, "Standard Test Methods and Definitions for Mechanical Testing of Steel Products," ASTM International, West Conshohocken, PA, 2012 www.astm.org.
16. ASTM Standard E8, "Standard Test Method for Tension Testing of Metallic Materials," ASTM International, West Conshohocken, PA, 2011 www.astm.org.
17. GMH Engineering. (1996). *DataBRICK Data Acquisition System Reference Manual.* Orem, UT.
18. SAE International. (1995 March). *SAE J211/1, Instrumentation for Impact Test—Part 1 Electronic Instrumentation.* Warrendale, PA.
19. Treichel, T., "Specific Locations of Damage and Lading Losses on Tank Heads and Shells," RSI-AAR Railroad Tank Car Safety Research and Test Project Report RA-06-04 (2007).

Appendix A. Estimates of Labor, Material and Capital Equipment for Manufacturing

In an effort to develop a framework to estimate the cost of side protection panels for railroad tank cars, CMI performed an analysis of the manufacturing costs and capital investments required to produce panels in annual volumes of 10k, 20k, and 40k in order to highlight any value of large-scale production.

The study also captured the projected costs for various retrofit panel strategies covering varying portions of the sides of a rail car; all of the sides (100 percent), all but the section around the manway (86 percent), only the bottom (50 percent) and only sections adjacent to the wheels (33 percent). The schematics shown in Figure 54 are representative of the locations on the tank shell in which accident data have been collected [19]. Moreover, the accident data indicate that the bottom half of the tank is more likely to be impacted and punctured than the top.

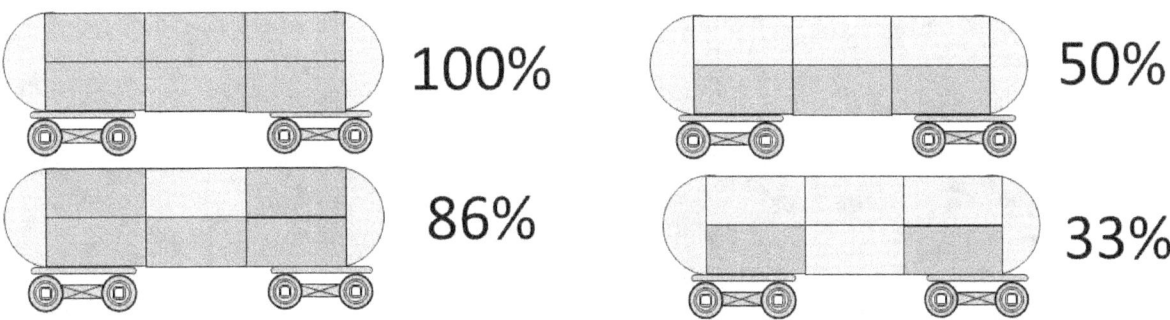

Figure 54. Various tank car coverage strategies

Panel Design Assumptions
Costs were estimated for panels designed and constructed the same way that they were manufactured for the test performed at the Transportation Technology Center, using a solid cold rolled 1010 carbon steel 0.120-inch thick front face sheet, standard 3-inch diameter tube with a 0.086-inch wall thickness, and a series of 3-inch wide 1010 steel 0.120-inch thick strips spaced 6 inches apart on the back. The tubes are attached to the front face sheet using GMAW plug welds every three inches and to the rear strips using GMAW plug welds with the same spacing. The tubes are not welded to each other. Some non-structural tack welding between the tubes is used during assembly to facilitate the manufacturing process.

In a full-scale production environment, it is assumed that the panels would likely be retrofitted to the tank cars in the same facility in which they were manufactured; however, this study concentrates on the manufacturing of the protective panels and their attachment systems only. Because carbon steel corrodes easily, a coating process was included in the study. Conventional spray painting will not provide adequate corrosion protection due to geometry of the tube core. The coating process included for this cost study could be either the addition of a protective layer of paint using a full immersion dip coating process or a galvanizing line. Both coating systems are assumed to require similar capital investment and direct labor content.

For the purpose of this analysis, it is further assumed that the panels are all the same size. A number of panel dimensions were considered, and it was decided that the optimum panel size would be approximately 7.5 feet by 6.25 feet. At this panel size, a standard CNC punch press can be used to cut the plug weld holes in the front face sheet, and the weight of the panel would be approximately 800 pounds which can be manipulated with conventional material handling equipment. With panels of this size, twelve panels would cover each side of a tank car.

Panel Manufacturing Assumptions
Figure 55 shows a flow chart representing the manufacturing process described in this section. The 1010 steel front face sheet material and tubes would be received from the mill cut to size. The rear strips would be cut in-house from a 3-inch wide coil of 1010 steel. The holes for plug welding would be cut into the front face sheet using a CNC punch. The rear strips would have plug holes punched on a progressive die during the process in which the strip material is straightened and cut to length. The tubes would be degreased prior to assembly to facilitate joining and make finishing of the assembly easier later in the production cycle. Both the face sheet and the rear strips would be rolled to the required curvature using a three roller mill large enough to accommodate a 7.5-foot wide face sheet.

Custom-made fixturing would be used during welding. These fixtures would be on tracks so that they could be moved in and out of the robotic welding cell. All setup would be done on the fixtures while they are outside the welding cell. Once the setup is completed, the parts would be moved into the cell for joining and then moved back out for additional setup. The first weld fixture would be designed to accept the tubular core and to position the rear strips accurately. Its surface would be concave with a radius that when the tubes and strips were loaded would achieve the required curvature of the inside, train car side, of the assembly. Both the tubes and strips would be loaded on the fixture manually with the assistance of a jib crane. The tubes would be tacked to each other in the assembly area using manual welding to reduce movement during robotic plug welding. When the assembly was ready for welding, it would be moved into the weld cell where two welding robots would plug weld the strips to the tubes. The plug welding of the assembly is the most time-intensive portion of the manufacturing operation. As currently designed, the panel will require 360 plug welds to attach the strips to the tubes which, using two robots simultaneously, would take approximately 24 minutes. Once welding is completed, the assembly still on the weld fixture would be moved out of the weld cell. A bridge crane would then be used to take the assembly off of the concave fixture, turn it over, and position it on a convex fixture. Using the overhead crane again, the front face sheet would be positioned on top of the assembly. The fixture and assembly would then be moved back into a robotic welding cell where two robots would plug weld the face sheet to the tubes using another 360 welds, which again would require 24 minutes. All plug welding would be done using GMAW. The final step in the panel manufacturing process would be cleaning and coating the panels with a protective layer to inhibit corrosion. Because the tubes would need corrosion protection on their inside surface, the coating method requires complete immersion of the panel in the coating. Dip painting or galvanizing are two potential methods that have similar capital and direct labor costs.

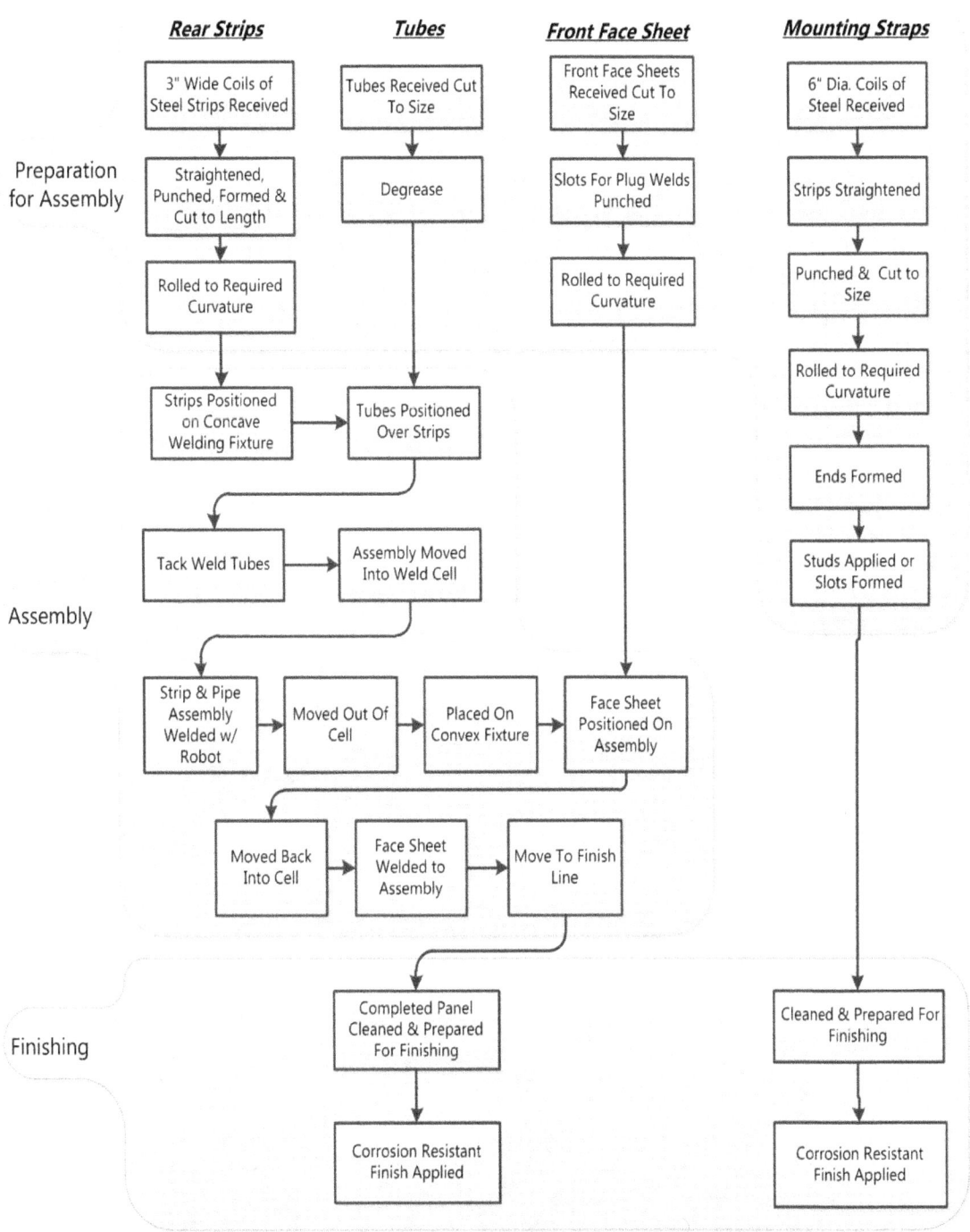

Rear Strips

3" Wide Coils of Steel Strips Received

Straightened, Punched, Formed & Cut to Length

Rolled to Required Curvature

Strips Positioned on Concave Welding Fixture

Tack Weld Tubes

Tubes

Tubes Received Cut To Size

Degrease

Tubes Positioned Over Strips

Assembly Moved Into Weld Cell

Front Face Sheet

Front Face Sheets Received Cut To Size

Slots For Plug Welds Punched

Rolled to Required Curvature

Mounting Straps

6" Dia. Coils of Steel Received

Strips Straightened

Punched & Cut to Size

Rolled to Required Curvature

Ends Formed

Studs Applied or Slots Formed

Strip & Pipe Assembly Welded w/ Robot

Moved Out Of Cell

Placed On Convex Fixture

Face Sheet Positioned On Assembly

Moved Back Into Cell

Face Sheet Welded to Assembly

Move To Finish Line

Completed Panel Cleaned & Prepared For Finishing

Corrosion Resistant Finish Applied

Cleaned & Prepared For Finishing

Corrosion Resistant Finish Applied

Preparation for Assembly

Assembly

Finishing

Figure 55. Railroad Tank Car Protective Panel and Mounting Strap Processing

57

Panel Attachment Assumptions

Ideally, the panels should be attached to the railroad tank car with minimal or no rework of the tank car itself, a goal that could be realized by employing a series of bands around the tank car to which the panels are "attached". One series of bands would be wrapped around the car over the existing steel jacket which currently protects the insulation layer. These bands would be positioned so that the panels could be "attached" to them by stud welding the panels to the straps or forming hooks into the straps, Figure 56. The panels would be hung on these mounting configurations and then held in place by a second set of straps which would be wrapped around the tank car overtop the protective panels. At each location at which the curved sides of the protective panels would abut one another, wider straps would be employed. These wider straps would be used to secure the edges of two panels. This is not illustrated in Figure 56.

The straps would be manufactured using 1010 steel coil stock 0.1875-inch thick and 6 inches wide. The strap material would be straightened, cut to size, and then rolled to the desired curvature. These straps would have holes punched in their ends. The ends would then be bent 90 degrees using a press brake so that a tensioning bolt could be used to tighten them to the tank car. If the hook method were used, the hooks would be formed at the same time that the punch pierced the holes in the ends. Figure 56 illustrates the proposed hook method to attach panels to the tank cars. If studs are used, the studs would be attached after the ends were formed. Because the mounting strap cost using either method would be similar and the cost of these straps is not significant, all cost projections assume using the stud welded straps.

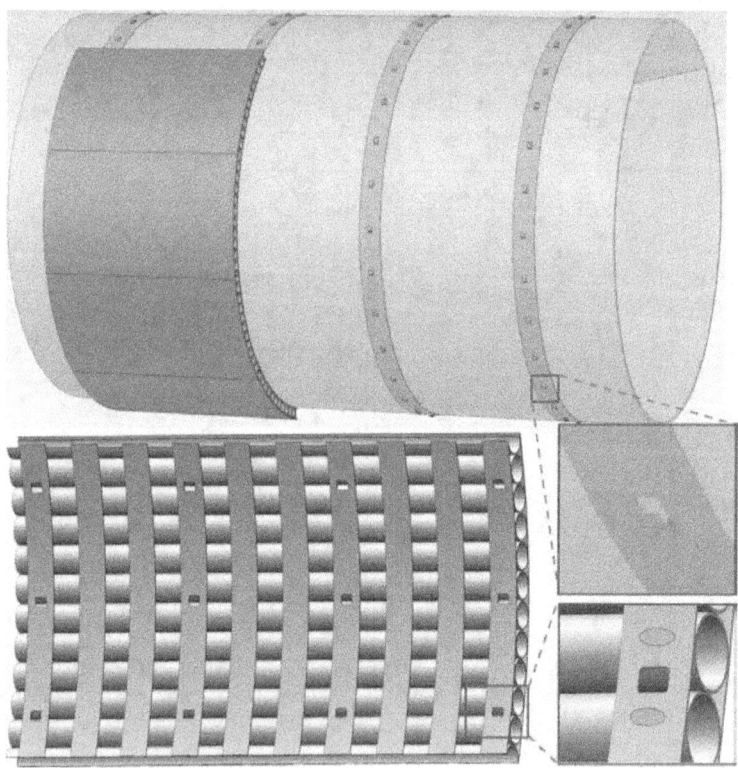

Figure 56. Demonstration of Attachment Scheme

Costing Assumptions
Calculations for the costs of the panels have been based on the following assumptions:

Railroad Tank Car

Tank Length – Assume 3-Foot Deep Heads	43.901	feet
Length of Tank to be Protected	37.901	feet
Tank Width	8.375	feet
Car Width w/ 4-Inch Insulation	9.042	feet
Tank Wall Thickness	0.777	inches
1010 Carbon Steel Cost	0.850	$/pound
Regular Core Tube Cost	1.500	$/foot
Individual Panel Width	6.30	feet
Individual Panel Height-Circumference	7.52	feet

Panel & Mounting Strap Information

Outer Face Sheet	0.120	inches
Pipe Diameter	3.00	inches
Pipe Wall	0.083	inches
Pipe Weight per Foot	2.599	pound/foot
Inner Face Sheet – Strips	0.120	inches
Mounting Strap – Inner	0.1875	inches
Mounting Strap – Outer	0.1875	inches

Cost Estimates
Estimated costs were projected for manufacturing tube core tank car protective panels measuring 7.5 feet by 6.25 feet with required mounting hardware at production rates of 10,000, 20,000, and 40,000 panels per year. In addition, estimates were generated for the capital investment required to support these annual production volumes (Table 14). Although panels and mounting straps would be sold and used in multiple quantities and not sold individually, the cost of one panel would be approximately $885 and the average cost of a mounting strap would be $184.

Table 14. Cost Estimates for Panel and Mounting Hardware

	10,000 Panels per Year	20,000 Panels per Year	40,000 Panels per Year
Panel Materials	$13,395	$12,725	$12,343
Mounting Straps	$1,274	$1,210	$1,174
Manufacturing Labor @ $20 per Hour	$3,106	$3,044	$2,983
Burden – 120% of Labor	$3,727	$3,653	$3,580
Margin – 5%	$1,075	$1,032	$1,004
Estimated Panel and Mounting Hardware per Car	$22,577	$21,664	$21,084
Capital Investment	$2,779,750	$3,666,650	$5,832,475
Breakeven – Panels	2,586	3,554	5,809
Breakeven – Months of Production	16	11	9

Labor costs will be relatively inelastic as production volumes increase. Most of the available manufacturing economies of scale will have already been achieved at the 10,000-panel per year level. For this reason, a manufacturing volume increase to 20,000 and 40,000 panels per year will represent only a minor efficiency improvement, a 2-percent drop in labor cost each time the volumes double. Increased volume will have a slightly greater impact on the material costs. A 5-percent decrease in material cost has been assumed if production increases from 10,000 to 20,000 panels per year and an additional 3 percent if the volume increases to 40,000 panels. Detailed labor, material, and capital equipment cost estimates are provided below.

Table 15. Labor Estimate for Panel Manufacturing

Plug Weld Both Sides & Use Robot

Panel Size – 6.3' x 7.5' w/ 3" Tube

	Minutes To Complete Step	Minutes per Piece	Pieces per Panel	People Required	Minutes per Panel
Rear Face Sheet - Strips - 12 per Panel					
Receive Coil 3" Wide, 120" Thick 1010 Steel Coil 712' Long (One Coil = Strips for 8 Panels)	30	3.75	1	1	4
Load Coil on Line and Set Up	30	3.75	1	2	8
Straighten, Punch, and Shear Strips	1	1	12	1	12
Roll to Required Curvature	3	3	12	1	36
Front Face Sheet					
Receive 60 Pieces	30	0.5	1	1	1
Set Up Face Sheet on Punch Press	6	6	1	2	12
Punch Slots – One Every 6"~360 Slots	0.05	0.05	360	1	18
Roll to Required Curvature	20	20	1	2	40
Tube					
Receive 1200 Pieces	60	0.05	30	1	2
Degrease, Clean, Dry, and Move to Line	1	1	30	1	30
Assembly Plug Weld					
Position Tube	1	1	30	2	60
Lay Strips	1	1	12	2	24
Tack Tube – Both Sides	0.25	0.25	60	1	15
Plug Weld the Strips w/ 2 Robots	0.067	2	12	1	24
Flip Panel	5	5	1	2	10
Place and Line Up Front Face Sheet	10	10	1	2	20
Tack Face Sheet to Tubes	0.25	0.25	60	1	15
Plug Weld Face Sheet to Tubes (2 Robots)	0.067	24	1	1	24
Remove Assembly	10	10	1	1	10
Clean & Dip					
Dip Assembly in Cleaning Solution	5	5	1	1	5
Coat Assembly	20	20	1	1	20
				Total	388 Minutes
					6.47 Hours

Table 16. Labor Estimate for Mounting Strap Manufacturing
Assumes Using Straps with Weld Studs

	Minutes to Complete Step	Minutes per Piece	Pieces per Panel	People Required	Minutes per Panel	
Straps						
Receive 10 Coils 12" Wide 0.1875" Thick 1010 Steel Coil 150' Long (One Coil = 6 Strips)	6	1	10	1	10	
Load Coil On Line and Set Up	15	2.5	10	1	25	
Receive 10 Coils 6" Wide 0.1875" Thick 1010 Steel Coil 150' Long (One Coil = 6 Strips)	6	1	4	1	4	
Load Coil on Line and Set Up	15	2.5	4	2	20	
Straighten, Punch, and Shear Strips	0.5	1	14	1	14	
Roll to Required Curvature	1	1	14	1	14	
Form Ends	1	1	28	1	28	
				Total	**115**	**Minutes**
					1.92	**Hours**

Table 17. Detailed Material Cost and Weight Calculations

	Height (Top to Bottom) Ft	Width (Side to Side) Ft	Thickness In	Studs Qty @ $1 each	Pcs	Total Weight	Waste	Cost
Panel – Each								
Top Face Sheets	7.52	6.32	0.120			234	0.00%	$199
Bottom Face Sheets – Strips	6.58	0.25	0.120		13	105	5.00%	$84
Core Tube	6.32	0.25			28	460	0.00%	$265
Totals						799		$558
Straps – Each								
Straps against the Tank – Single	0.50	28.41	0.1875	12		67	5.00%	$71
Straps against the Tank – Double	1.00	28.41	0.1875	24		133	5.00%	$143
Outer Strap – Single	0.50	29.98	0.1875			58	5.00%	$51
Outer Strap – Double	1.00	29.98	0.1875			115	5.00%	$103

Table 18. Projected Capital Equipment Requirements for Protective Panel Manufacturing

Process	Part Processed	Equipment Description	Base Cost	Freight & Setup	Total Cost	Qty of Machines	$	Qty of Machines	$	Qty of Machines	$
Feed Strips	Rear Face / Hold Down Straps	Payoff	$500		$500	3	$1,500	3	$1,500	3	$1,500
Coil Feed	Rear Face / Hold Down Straps	Coil Feeder	$6,000		$6,000	1	$6,000	1	$6,000	1	$6,000
Straighten Coil	Rear Face / Hold Down Straps	Cooper Weymouth 6"	$4,950	$1,000	$5,950	1	$5,950	1	$5,950	1	$5,950
Punch Holes - Strips	Rear Face	Model PM2-20 Minster	$24,500	$6,125	$30,625	1	$30,625	1	$30,625	1	$30,625
Shear	Rear Face / Hold Down Straps	Small Shear	$15,000	$3,750	$18,750	1	$18,750	1	$18,750	1	$18,750
Roll	Face Sheets / Hold Down Straps	Bend Parts To Shape	$25,000	$6,250	$31,250	2	$62,500	3	$93,750	4	$125,000
Move	Raw Materials	Forklift	$17,000	$4,250	$21,250	2	$42,500	3	$63,750	4	$85,000
Move	Assembly	EMH Overhead Crane 3 Ton	$30,000	$10,500	$40,500	2	$81,000	3	$121,500	5	$202,500
Move	Move parts	Catelivered Hoist	$1,200	$400	$1,600	8	$12,800	12	$19,200	24	$38,400
Punch Holes - Front Face	Front Face Sheet	Turret Press	$149,500	$37,375	$186,875	1	$186,875	1	$186,875	2	$373,750
Tacking	Assembly	Mig Welder	$48,000	$2,000	$50,000	4	$200,000	8	$400,000	12	$600,000
Robot Weld	Assembly	Motoman Robot - 2 per Line	$165,000	$41,250	$206,250	4	$825,000	6	$1,237,500	12	$2,475,000
Hold Panel	Assembly	Convex Jig Carts	$15,000		$15,000	6	$90,000	10	$150,000	18	$270,000
Hold Panel	Assembly	Concave Jig Carts	$15,000		$15,000	6	$90,000	10	$150,000	18	$270,000
Bend Straps	Straps	Cincinnati Press Brake	$42,000	$10,500	$52,500	1	$52,500	1	$52,500		
Bend Straps	Straps	Press w/ progressive dies	$100,000	$15,000	$115,000					1	$115,000
Clean Raw Parts	All	Degrees Bath	$45,000	$11,250	$56,250	2	$112,500	2	$112,500	2	$112,500
Finishing Line	Complete line	Finishing Line	$700,000	$175,000	$875,000	1	$875,000	1	$875,000	1	$875,000
Air	Plant	Compressed Air source	$25,000	$6,250	$31,250	1	$31,250	1	$31,250	2	$62,500
Misc	Plant	Mics Hand Trucks, Racks and Tools	$50,000	$5,000	$55,000	1	$55,000	2	$110,000	3	$165,000
					Totals		$2,779,750		$3,666,650		$5,832,475

Assuming the fabrication of 10,000 panels per year, the cost of the four different levels of protection are as shown in Table 19. All coverage strategies, except the 33 percent coverage, require approximately the same amount of mounting hardware. Because the 33 percent coverage requires no mounting hardware in the center section of the tank car, the mounting hardware requirement would be less.

Table 19. Options for Tank Car Coverage

Option		All Sides Covered	All Sides Except Manway Area	Only Bottom Half	Only Above Truck Assemblies
Percent Coverage		100%	86%	50%	33%
Number of Panels		24	20	12	8
Number of Mounting Straps	Wide Outer	5	5	5	1
	Narrow Outer	2	2	2	4
	Wide Inner	5	5	5	1
	Narrow Inner	2	2	2	4
Materials	Panels	$13,395	$11,162	$6,697	$4,465
	Straps	$1,274	$1,274	$1,274	$697
Manufacturing Labor @ $20/hour	Panels	$3,106	$2,588	$1,553	$1,035
	Straps	$537	$537	$537	$383
Burden	120% of Labor	$4,371	$3,750	$2,508	$1,702
Margin	5%	$1,134	$966	$628	$414
Estimate: Cost of Panel and Mounting Hardware per Car		$23,817	$20,277	$13,197	$8,697

NOTE: Based on 100% coverage figures, a single panel would cost approximately $885 and a mounting strap $184.

Future Considerations

These cost estimates for manufacturing the protective panels assumed similar production methods as those used to fabricate a single sample panel that was tested at the Transportation Technology Center on May 18, 2011. For example, plug welds were used every 6 inches to attach the front face sheet and rear strips to the tubular core. This joining process is time-intensive even with two relatively high speed welding robots working in tandem. The 7.5-foot by 6.25-foot panel would require 720 plug welds, 360 on each side, which require a total of 48 minutes to complete. It is recommended that further study be performed to investigate lowering the cost of these protective panels by reducing the welding time. One potential cost saving strategy would be to decrease the number of welds by increasing the spacing between them. Another possibility is to use edge welds at the interface between the pipe and strips which could potentially reduce welding time. Both efficiency improvements warrant study before evaluating the cost effectiveness of this protective paneling system.

In addition, the attachment methods proposed in this study are conceptual and were included to establish estimated costs for attachment. These attachment methods would need to be built and tested along with other possible methods of attachment prior to finalizing the tank car protection concept.

Appendix B. Protective Panel Attachments to Tank Car

At the beginning of this task, the project team suggested investigating tank car panel attachment methods. Stud welding technique was identified as a potential method. Accordingly, the CMI team worked with a stud welding tool manufacturer to further investigate the process. To attach the sandwich panels to the tank car body, studs would be welded to the outer body of the tank car so that the panels could then be bolted to the studs. Although this method was eventually not selected for attaching the impact panel to the chlorine tank, the results are presented below.

Study Welding Study

TC128-B is the standard steel used in the construction of the tank car bodies; therefore, stud welding to the TC128-B steel was investigated. For this study, $\frac{7}{8}$-inch diameter studs were welded to 0.453-inch thick normalized TC128-B plate. The stud welding technique used was the capacitance discharge method performed at Nelson Stud Welding's test lab. Two of the samples were tensile tested to failure. Both samples failed in the stud, at 29,000 pounds and 30,400 pounds of tension, and showed no distortion in the weld area. In addition, weld adhesion was tested by bending a welded stud 90 degrees. No failure occurred in the weld area, but there was evidence of failure initiating in the stud itself between some of the threads, as shown in Figure 57.

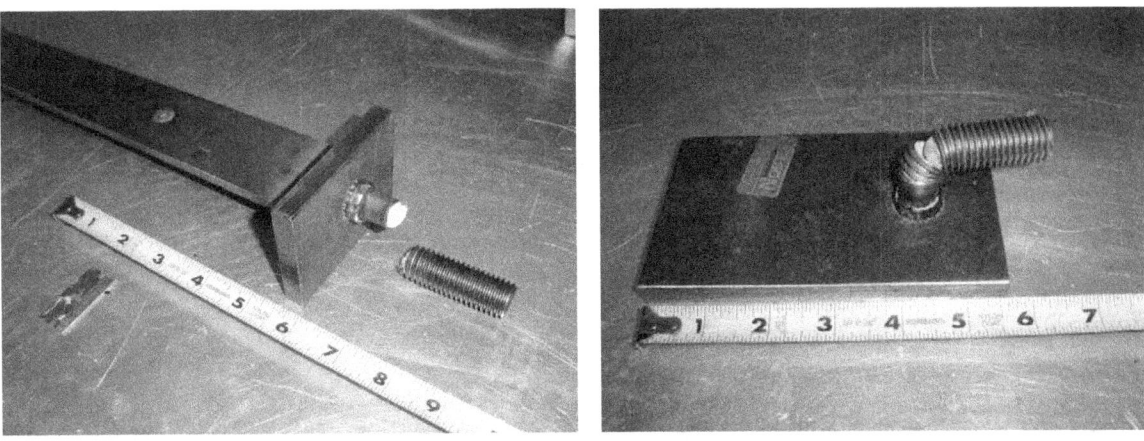

Figure 57. Stud Weld after Tensile Test (left) and Bend Test (right)

In view of this positive preliminary test result, it appeared that stud welding to a TC128-B pressure vessel could be achieved without requiring post heat treatment. In order to verify this, the stud welds were sectioned axially through the center of the studs, polished, and etched in 2 percent nital; the cross-sections were then examined metallographically. TC128-B has a microstructure of banded ferritic steel—with a ferrite grain size of 10 µm or less—and a pearlite phase dispersed into it. In the rolled condition, the pearlite stringers are elongated in the rolling direction. The stud bolt blank is a forged low carbon steel material. Its microstructure is a mixture of banded ferrite and pearlite with a ferrite grain size of about 30 µm.

A composite micrograph of the cross section of the stud welds is shown in Figure 58, illustrating the TC128-B base metal on the top and the stud bolt cross-section on the bottom. There were HAZs in both the steels; in addition, between the HAZs, where the stud was plunged into the base metal, there was a "mushy" zone. The mushy zone was overetched making it difficult to identify the phases present; however, it appeared to contain lower transformation products. In the HAZ in the TC128-B steel, the stringer pearlite phase had transformed to martensite, which is a hard, plate-like structure (Figure 25). This phase is brittle with internal stresses that can lead to weld cracking.

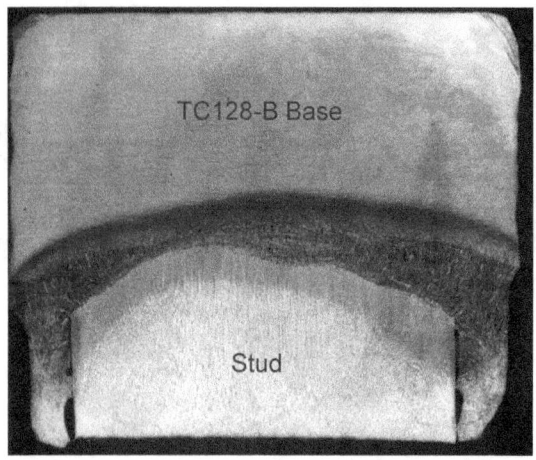

Figure 58. Cross Section of Weld

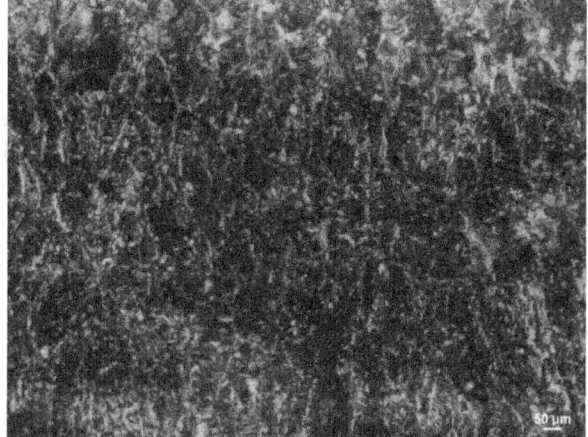

Figure 59. HAZ in TC128-B Steel

The HAZ in the stud area is shown in Figure 60. Since the carbon content in this steel is higher than that of TC128-B, the dissolved carbon was transformed into bainite and spherodized pearlite. The transformed product in the microstructure will contribute residual stresses leading to structural weakness and cracking; therefore, a post stress relieving treatment is necessary. The base metal microstructure of the stud bolt, typical of high carbon ferritic and pearlitic steel, is shown in Figure 61. The stress relieving treatment will normalize the residual stresses and modify the microstructures of both martensite in the TC128-B steel and bainite in the plain carbon steel in order to provide more ductility and better toughness.

Figure 60. HAZ in Stud Bolt Region

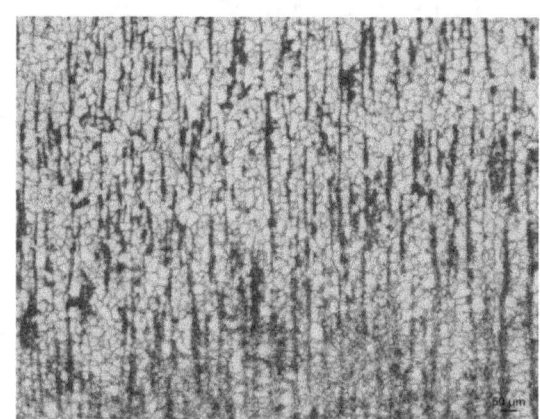

Figure 61. Microstructure of Stud Bolt

The hardness of the stud and the TC128-B base plates were 170 and 200 HV (at 200-gram indenter load), respectively, consistent with their pearlite (carbon) contents. The "mushy" zone had a peak hardness of 495 HV, and the HAZs transitioned from base metal hardness to 300 HV for the stud and 380 HV for the TC128-B plate. The higher hardness is attributable to the lower transformation products.

In order to relieve the stress and improve the ductility, the weld requires post heat treatment. A temper heat treatment at 1150 °F for ½ to 1 hour is recommended. Based on this study, it is recommended that the studs be attached to the tank car before the tank car is stress relieved.

Alternate Attachment Schemes
Since the protective panels may be retrofitted onto existing tank cars, stress relieving the entire tank car is not practical. Other attachment methods will need to be developed. One method proposed by CMI is to wrap straps around tank cars that have either studs or brackets to which the panels could be attached. For a retrofit, in order to save weight and cost, only the areas of the tank car which, based on history, are the most likely to be punctured would be protected. Since the bottom half of the tank is the primary region that needs protection [19], it is possible that studs could be welded to existing brackets that are used for the braking system. The panels could then be attached to those studs. An outer strap may act as a hoop or belt on the exterior of the panel to provide additional tension to hold the panel in place.

Future Considerations
Based on the work completed during the 3-year project and, in particular, the results from the manufacturing and testing of the full-scale panel, the following recommendations were compiled:
- Spot welding should not be utilized to manufacture the panels.
- The two mating fixtures on which the curved panel was fabricated offer a solid manufacturing approach for building a panel with a defined radius.
- Further study is recommended to decrease weld time by (1) decreasing density of welds and/or (2) using edge welds on strip in place of plug welds.
- To prevent the lateral movement of tubes, a half tube is positioned on each end of the panel.

Abbreviations and Acronyms

AAR	Association of American Railroads
AISI	American Iron and Steel Institute
ATLSS	Advanced Technology for Large Structural Systems
ASTM	American Society for Testing and Materials
CMI	Cellular Materials International, Inc.
EWI	Edison Welding Institute
FRA	Federal Railroad Administration
GMAW	gas metal arc welding
HAZ	heat affected zone
HD	high definition
HS	high speed
HSLA	high strength low alloy
SBIR	Small Business Innovation Research
TIH	toxic inhalation hazard
TTCI	Transportation Technology Center, Inc.
VTRC	Virginia Transportation Research Council

www.ingramcontent.com/pod-product-compliance
Lightning Source LLC
Chambersburg PA
CBHW080433290526
45791CB00008BA/2476

9 781499 123180